COMBATING SOCIAL EXCLUSION IN UNI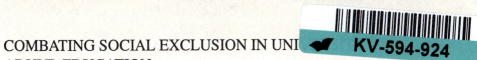 KV-594-924
ADULT EDUCATION

Combating Social Exclusion in University Adult Education

JULIA PREECE
University of Surrey

Ashgate

Aldershot • Brookfield USA • Singapore • Sydney

Published by
Ashgate Publishing Ltd
Gower House
Croft Road
Aldershot
Hants GU11 3HR
England

Ashgate Publishing Company
Old Post Road
Brookfield
Vermont 05036
USA

Ashgate website: http://www.ashgate.com

British Library Cataloguing in Publication Data
Preece, Julia
    Combating social exclusion in university adult education. -
    (Interdisciplinary research series in ethnic, gender and
    class relations)
    1.Education, Higher - Great Britain 2.Adult education -
    Great Britain 3.Social isolation - Great Britain
    I.Title
    378.4'1

Library of Congress Catalog Card Number: 99-73641

ISBN 0 7546 1150 7

Printed and bound by Athenaeum Press, Ltd.,
Gateshead, Tyne & Wear.

Contents

Preface

> We need to know much more about learning activities and opportunities throughout life, in all sorts of setting, particularly in respect of those currently under-represented in lifelong learning (Fryer 1997: 37).

This is a story of one university continuing education department's involvement with adults most on the margins of formal education. It exposes the rhetoric behind the words 'higher education for everyone able to benefit', particularly in a lifelong learning context, and underlines the need to rethink some of higher education's criteria for excellence. The book's argument is that more should mean different and also inclusive.

Thirty community learners with diverse backgrounds tell their personal histories of how their respective education systems and social expectations pigeon-holed them and their learning throughout their lives. Experiences of professional as well as local attitudes towards employment, disability, culture, ethnicity, gender and class have ultimately impinged on what individuals chose to do and what they thought they were entitled to as adults. In spite of this influence some people gave examples of independent learning which revealed latent and unrecognised intellectual talent from the most unexpected corners.

The book contrasts the depth of people's learning on specially designed community courses with more traditional institutional criteria for 'quality', 'higher' and 'appropriate curriculum'. The community learners responses to their targeted programmes show what can be achieved when people's cultural and social values are taken into account.

Although the context for this study is higher education (or more specifically, university continuing education), many of its findings have relevance to a wide range of educational institutions. The book challenges, for instance, some of the assumptions surrounding recent proposals to widen participation. It places the blame for non-participation on educational institutions rather than the learner. The decisions made by education providers about curriculum, style of provision and type of teacher often exacerbate the divide, into adulthood, between those who participate in formal education and those who do not.

The study developed from my own practitioner remit to provide courses in community settings for marginalised social groups. My experience of trying to justify the appropriateness of this work to my university employer provided me with the question - why do some adults remain with community courses and not transfer their enthusiasms for learning into traditional continuing education provision? The concept of social exclusion as: 'exclusion from the systems which facilitate social integration' (Howarth & Kenway 1998: 80) only partially answers this question.

The first part of this book describes the context for my work - why I was appointed, the changing political scene during my employment and the relationship of my work to similar projects in other universities. I follow this with an explanation of the theoretical framework which helped me explain the issues around participation for my community contacts and for my continuing education department. The second part of the book describes conversations and struggles within my department alongside almost parallel struggles and opinions from academics in three other universities. There is then a short account of each community learner's personal history, contextualised by their local cultural and social environments. Chapters six and seven describe and explain their different facets of exclusion. In chapters eight and nine the learners identify learning which was important for them and explain why they valued the community courses. Chapter ten looks at how different educational experiences contribute to shaping and reshaping the developing self. I argue that 'non participants' in formal education are indeed active participants when their own needs, values and social networks are recognised. Their absence from the mainstream is due to attitudes from within institutions, rather than a lack of interest in learning amongst the marginalised. I conclude with some recommendations for future practice.

This study originated as a PhD thesis. It has been substantially re-written, up-dated and slightly re-focused to take account of recent debates concerning social exclusion and social capital.

Acknowledgements

This book would not have been possible without the cooperation of several, anonymous, academic colleagues and the thirty adult learners who so freely gave so much information about themselves. I owe them all a debt of gratitude.

I should also like to thank Ron Barnett, Gill Nicholls and Peter Jarvis for their support, advice and encouragement in helping me turn my research into its present book form.

1 Setting the scene: the wider political context

In 1991 I was appointed to a university continuing education department. My role was to 'reach out' to marginalised social groups in the region and provide short courses which were of university standard. Such groups would be identified largely as people who have minimal initial education and from socio economic groups four and five (skilled, semi skilled or manual workers); in particular, having a disability, being of minority ethnic background or being of retirement age (Sargant 1992, 1997, Metcalf 1993, McGivney 1990, Martin, White & Meltzer 1989). It was a similar project to that undertaken by a number of universities and came nationally to be known as 'work to counter educational disadvantage' (UCACE 1992). I was to bridge the gap between 'non participants' and the primarily white, middle class and well educated clientele in the department's traditional programme of short, non-award bearing courses for the general public. The traditional courses were taught by academics, usually on topics which related to the subjects (disciplines) of university departments and were known as liberal adult education (LAE). Although non award bearing, the level of such provision was generally considered to be comparable with the first year of a university undergraduate course. Associated study expectations varied but it was implicitly assumed that people who attended would pursue their interest in the subject with further, independent reading.

Over the next few years funding criteria changed. LAE courses became award bearing. That is each twenty or thirty hour course would now carry credit points for completed assignments, which could be accumulated towards a Certificate. The Certificate was equivalent to the first year of undergraduate study. Courses now needed to be validated by university committees and secure support from relevant 'cognate' subject departments within the institution. My work became separately funded in 1995 under a four year initiative to 'widen participation' in higher education. The community courses would remain non award bearing, though some carried an optional 'Access' level credit (equivalent in standard to A level, the required entry qualification for university study).

My community education activities succeeded in developing a substantial programme of courses for a wide range of under-represented groups. I adopted a strategy which is well rehearsed by community educators (Ward and Taylor 1986, Lovett 1982, Thompson 1980, McGivney 1990). Figure one shows this strategy as a diagram. It entailed collaborating with small voluntary organisations and local education providers. In some areas I employed a part time 'role model' link worker - someone who had a similar social or cultural background to their local community. Course content would be discussed between myself, the link worker and local organisations who had a particular group of participants in mind. The participants' educational backgrounds would influence both teaching style and curriculum materials. Most of the courses would also be taught by role model tutors, or people who had longstanding credibility or empathy with their learners. Some courses would be taught bilingually, others would be taught by people with relevant experience, rather than particular academic qualifications. Most of the subjects or topics were chosen by community leaders or the participants themselves. The teaching required a critical, analytical approach, but not necessarily with reference to substantial pieces of written work. Courses were rarely advertised other than through locally known routes for members of particular communities and would be provided at a time, place and pace to suit each learner group.

Figure 1 The community education strategy

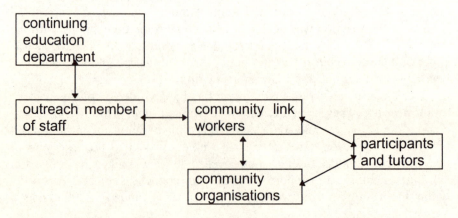

The majority of participants would attend more than one community course. Often participants shared some sort of social or cultural identity outside of an interest in the course topic. Few of these participants subsequently elected to take part in the department's main LAE programme or other mainstream provision, and of those that did, most dropped out

2

before course completion. In contrast, the majority of LAE, now credit, participants already had professional qualifications or degrees and partook in the main programme for personal interest or with professional updating goals.

The evolution of two separate strands of provision (the mainstream credit and community courses) raised a number of ideological and philosophical questions within the department, and occasionally outside the department, as to the precise nature of the community activities and their appropriateness for university provision. Discussions with people who had similar roles in other university continuing education departments suggested that these concerns had wider applicability than just within my institution. The study which provided the material for this book developed during a period of intensive debate about differences between the department's main credit provision and the community courses. This in turn coincided with the department's own critical period of funding changes and consequent interactions with other parts of the university. The ensuing debates produced some recurrent issues. They are identified here under the following themes:

- the notion of critical analysis in higher education and its relationship to text based learning and teaching
- a perception of the adult learner as a particular kind of person
- the idea of 'appropriate' curriculum content and tutors for higher education
- the vision of widening access as a one-way process of bringing people 'into the fold'
- an assumption that higher education is all-embracing, objective and value-free.

In the process of defending my corner regarding the nature and purpose of the community courses I decided to find a way of identifying what I saw as the cultural differences between the department's institutional attitudes and those of the learner groups with whom I was working. I involved three different social groups of participants from four geographical locations, plus their role model tutors or link workers. The course participants in particular would talk about their educational experiences and their views concerning university education. I also talked to academics who either had responsibility for similar community courses to mine or were employed to manage or teach the credit programme. In addition, departmental correspondence and other written exchanges within the university provided an academic backdrop, against which the book's main arguments are placed.

3

The above exchanges were taking place in a publications arena which was also discussing the nature of higher education, continuing education and its LAE heritage. Influencing some of these debates has been an increasing European focus on the vocational relevance of learning alongside a plethora of policy documents which attach great economic importance to ensuring everyone takes part in learning throughout their life. These debates have consequences for the people who took part in the community provision outlined in this book. The debates and current concepts for higher education therefore need to be rehearsed here briefly. The first issues to consider are: how higher education is perceived by the academic world; and the relationship between higher education and continuing education provision.

Higher education

Barnett, amongst others, has explored some common features of learning for a higher education student. He described these in 1988 as:

> The development of the student's intellectual skills or academic competencies ... critical abilities, especially the propensity to be self critical: the ability to analyse and evaluate relevant connections; the willingness to accept the rules of rational inquiry and the self motivation of the students, such as to go on learning and being self critical independently of any intrinsic influence (p.245).

These qualities have more to do with the nature of the learning experience than the matter of subject content. They are essentially about a type of learning which develops a certain type of learner. McNair (1995) has added to this list by suggesting that another essential quality of higher education learning is 'contesting knowledge' within certain rules of inquiry:

> The central experience of higher education is about learning how such contesting can be done within the established frameworks and gradually learning how to create new knowledge, to challenge established knowledge and test the frameworks for themselves (p.5).

Knowledge in this context is again more about a process of acquisition and use than specific content. These definitions pose both potential and problems for the accounts which follow. The concepts of 'critical', 'inquiry' and 'continuous learning', for instance, seem to be used in the literature as self defining norms for the university experience. Indeed they pervade most discussions about university education, whatever its form. Skilbeck and Connell (1996), for example, confirm that the essence of higher education is its focus on the critical spirit and recognition of the interconnectedness of knowledge, the ability to locate and evaluate information. They also see higher education as developing 'personal agency' and self awareness (pp 57-8).

I will argue, however, that university critical thinking takes place in a context which allows only certain view points, approved through authorised texts. New knowledge is allowed but only if it is derived in certain, approved ways - approved by those from within the system (primarily people who are white, male, able bodied and middle class). The contesting of knowledge identified by McNair is consequently self defining as it can only be done from within established frameworks and through the use of peer authorised texts. Knowledge therefore is narrowly defined by, and according to, the social and cultural milieu of those who already create it. Its process of critical appreciation also remains within its own boundaries, so much so that: 'Those who are situated in a particular paradigm have difficulty appreciating what is not defined as valuable within that paradigm' (Moghissi 1994: 229).

This notion of higher education, or indeed, formal education generally, is not without its critics. Usher and Edwards (1994) among others, question the historical premis for the established education system which must respond to today's world of uncertainty, pluralism and change:

> Historically, education can be seen as the vehicle by which modernity's grand narratives, the Enlightenment ideals of critical reason, individual freedom, progress and benevolent change, are substantiated and realised ...[as] the self motivated, self directing, rational subject, capable of exercising individual agency (Usher and Edwards 1994: 2).

They go on to suggest that the literature's definition of the learner needs to be reconceptualised to be more inclusive.

Aronowitz and Giroux (1991) critique more specifically the teaching process and the curriculum. They too are critical of how official texts produce boundaries for knowledge. They emphasise there are different terrains of knowledge and learning which are influenced by time, place, identity and power. They advocate a kind of teaching which: 'makes central to its project the recovery of these forms of knowledge and history that characterise alternate and oppositional others' (p.119). There are therefore signs that people are looking for new ways of weaving a path through modern day demands for increased higher education. Such demands are

5

often tied to a perceived responsiveness to industry and alongside challenges to university elitism so that a new culture of diversity can thrive within the mainstream. The NIACE (1993) policy discussion paper, for instance, emphasises the need to define new knowledge in new ways: 'The right of particular groups to define what is legitimate knowledge will increasingly be tested from a growing range of standpoints' (ibid: 15).

These debates are coming under increasing scrutiny as people discuss what kind of higher education is suitable for a mass system in a lifelong learning context. So, for example, McNair (1998), Scott (1997) and Watson and Taylor (1998) place a premium on the higher education teaching process. They emphasise that it should concentrate on encouraging the creation, rather than transmission of knowledge, with a recognition that adults now constitute the majority of the student population. They claim that the new higher education systems will need to be more flexible, completed in smaller units and more related to the world of work. Such systems are also likely to include a stronger focus on promoting general, transferable, higher learning skills such as the ability to apply knowledge and understanding (Cryer 1998). In the modern, unpredictable and uncertain world, knowledge rapidly gets out of date - hence the need for adaptability skills and systems which accommodate re-entry into study for all parts of the population.

The new world order for higher education, however, is rooted in a philosophy and tradition which has already defined what counts as knowledge - and even what are acceptable ways of acquiring new knowledge. This philosophy and tradition particularly underpins university adult education and takes its legacy from an embedded notion of liberal adult education (LAE). In the older universities this is provided through designated adult education departments. Although the nature of this provision in its purest sense is fading rapidly its rationale for what counts as a suitable university curriculum lingers on. It heritage therefore is still worth glossing over.

The liberal adult education heritage

Fieldhouse (1996) claims that the form, if not the content, of LAE can be traced back to early, 19th century working class adult education discussion groups which set the precedent for adult education as a dialogic, democratic exchange. These classes, he says, distinguished LAE from the more didactic tradition of state controlled vocational training.

Liberal education, taken in its broadest sense, was regarded as non partisan and pluralist in approach. Its aim was to avoid injudicious bias towards localised interests, to avoid a left wing slant, to work according to only recommended books and authors. The educational aim, as Raybould (1964) argued, was: 'more than the imparting of accurate information' (p.130). The emphasis was on learning as a cultural experience which was independent of social purpose and value free - but a learning which trained the mind to think and reflect. Elsey (1986) described this learning process as: 'examining ideas from different perspectives and dispassionate inquiry' (p.70).

It is these concepts which seem to have generated most debate. For instance, the possibility of 'dispassionate inquiry' as an exercise in objective analysis is challenged for its achievability at all: 'It is arguable that to be neutral or objective in the sense of being value-free is an impossibility for an adult educator' (Fieldhouse 1985: 23); and sometimes for its deliberate use as a: 'smoke screen to discriminate against Marxist and other socialist perspectives' (Fieldhouse 1985, introduction).

The rationale behind both claims seems embedded in an ideological conflict resulting from the growth of capitalism and alternative working class initiatives to challenge the social order upon which universities as elitist and privileged institutions were built. It is commonly argued, for instance (Simon 1990, Westwood and Thomas 1991, Fieldhouse 1996), that independent initiatives in the early 1900s to develop a curriculum of relevance for the working class were challenged as subversive and Marxist. The state's supported creation of the WEA in 1903 consequently emerged as an alternative higher education arm for the working classes. But they were granted state funding on condition they only accepted university lecturers as a teaching resource. This was in order to provide a 'stable' curriculum in competition with the more grass roots funded National Labour Colleges which developed around the same period. The views of the colleges were delegitimated as biased and partial, in contrast to the intellectual, and higher rationality, of abstract university thinking. The development of university LAE must therefore be understood from the perspective of its originators - a philanthropic minority of the ruling class - which necessarily had a vested interest in maintaining the status quo. Liberal education's position of objective and political neutrality is perceived by some as resistance to social action, because non-action and passive neutrality inevitably support the prevailing orthodoxies in society, which in themselves have built the system and its power structure (Thompson 1980). Consequently, it is argued, the liberal tradition itself already starts from a position of bias, whose own rules prevent a more equal distribution of values. A more constructive form of

7

learning, for instance, might include enquiry followed by direct action, drawing on people's own experiences, rather than simply acquired written information (Thompson 1980, Jackson 1980).

Whilst LAE retains its philosophical heritage in much non vocational adult education the past forty years have seen a continuous shift in policy and provision towards a vocationally oriented focus and more instrumental approach to learning. As a result university versions of vocational education have adopted a hybrid of liberal adult education, but within a more product oriented context. Indeed, the 1970s saw international organisations such as the OECD and UNESCO producing reports which created the impetus for a lifelong learning agenda. Their emphasis was on technology and vocationalism as a means of global integration (Hamilton 1996, Korsgaard 1997, Tuckett 1997). European White Papers have focused on promoting social inclusion through lifelong learning as a skills updating process whose goal is to develop flexible, mobile young people, able to adapt to a fast changing and increasingly interactive world (DGXXII, 1995). More recently the British Government's own Social Exclusion Unit has proposed strategies for neighbourhood renewal with an emphasis on education and training initiatives (1998).

Since 1995 UK LAE has lost its historical place as a distinctive, non award bearing feature of university part time study. A relatively recent term has been introduced to reflect the image of university adult education as an updating process. Continuing education (CE) is becoming almost synonymous with lifelong learning and both terms are used to describe current day university departments which make separate part-time provision for adults. CE's broad definition is generally understood to refer to part-time study for learners: 'other than those progressing directly to higher education from full time initial studies' (Slowey 1997: 196).

The question of who participates in the university experience, however, has remained problematic. Late twentieth century statistics regarding working class participation of all ages in higher education have changed relatively little since those early attempts via universities and the specific bridging remit of the WEA. In spite of an increased expansion of mainstream higher education from fifteen percent of the population to thirty percent in the last thirty years, the social class make up of learners has barely changed, particularly among adults (Sargant et al 1997, Dearing 1997). There is an increasing literature which challenges the university's abdication of responsibility for this trend, especially from the viewpoints of under-represented groups. Much of the criticisms revolve round the way universities teach, what they teach and how the learner is construed.

New challenges to continuing education

The 1990s saw a changing view of how the adult learner is constructed and portrayed. Parsons (1993) for instance, identified how women are made invisible in teaching situations through language use, attitudes and power relationships, all of which could have an effect on how women might participate in formal education. Other writers (Leicester 1993, Moghissi 1994, Lynch & O'Riordan 1998) draw attention to endemic prejudices within institutional infrastructures which actively work against facilitating participation from under-represented groups. Oliver (1990) for example remarks on how curriculum content in all teaching denies the disabled world a language or behaviour which can integrate with other life patterns: 'Education takes place in a context in which any understanding of the history and politics of disability is absent' (p.97). The result is an incoherent picture of knowledge and value-free education: 'In an attempt to be balanced and fair, adult educators have slanted their provision towards the dominant natural culture' (Hughes and Kennedy 1985: 165). In other words conventional liberal education may offer theoretical and abstract perspectives of the world but it barely challenges their applicability to real-life circumstances, nor does it encourage participants to question what is commonly regarded as normal.

These more recent views have seldom been tested empirically, particularly with regard to the curriculum or style of higher education and the influence of class, disability, long term unemployment or race on learning experiences.

So what have recent policy documents done to move us towards a more inclusive education system? It may be useful to look first at how social exclusion is being defined, particularly in relation to lifelong learning.

The current state of play: social exclusion and lifelong learning

There is a subtle link between current definitions of social exclusion and political measures which claim to tackle equity. Nineteen ninety seven to eight saw the publication of four major Government sponsored documents, together with a number of conferences and publications addressing the topic of social exclusion.

These publications make a strong political association between poverty, social exclusion and inequality (Oppenheim 1998, Clayton 1999). Social exclusion is also defined as multifaceted, rather than an end state. Oppenheim claims that social exclusion is a relational term which is really more about social processes which produce 'loss of status, power, self esteem and expectations' (p.15). Howarth and Kenway (1998) explain that these outcomes are brought about by 'exclusion from systems which facilitate social integration' (p.80). Social exclusion can therefore mean exclusion from the legal system, from the labour market, the welfare system, the family and community. Exclusion by these definitions is 'more than poverty'. It is linked to a notion of 'normal life' (Geddes 1997: 5-6). Duffy (1997) suggests that exclusion is brought about by a situation where rapid change overtakes the development of appropriate societal mechanisms to re-integrate people into the new world order. The consequences of this are defined by Saad (1997) as a three speed environment where the third speed population suffers from relative poverty, high dependency, none or little choice and poor services. They are, he says, the consequences of the failure of trickle down regeneration policy. Social exclusion, then is described as a state of being for certain sections of the population, underpinned primarily by their lack of access to the labour market and its associated contribution to society. Social inclusion is an attempt to 'normalise' the unemployed and disaffected. As such it legitimates the status quo of those systems which might otherwise be regarded as contributing to the very problem being addressed. The term social exclusion therefore is 'culturally defined, economically driven and politically motivated' (Barry 1998: 9). Policy addresses the issue through education and training provision. The connection between such definitions and the experiences of the community learners in this study indicates that neither definitions nor solutions are necessarily addressing the root issues behind an exclusionary society.

For some people, normalisation may well be an advantageous move beyond their current state of being. Rockhill (1996) states, however, that the political tactic of paying repeated lip service to the values of equity is effectively silencing those who are saying it is not happening. In terms of education and training one effect of new policies is to place the blame for non participation on the learner and normalise their involvement. The Kennedy report (1997), was the first of three successive reports which addressed, respectively further education (FE), higher education (HE) (Dearing 1997) and then more generally lifelong learning (Fryer 1997). They all offered a range of arguments in relation to widening participation. Kennedy emphasised the need to 'change public attitude' to learning, to 'create a positive attitude' (p.107). These statements effectively reinforce Rockhill's position. They ignore the possibility that it is the providers who do not view the learners positively enough. The Dearing (1997) higher education report also diminishes institutional responsibility for educational equity. This report claims that the prime causes of non participation 'lie outside of higher education' (paragraph 7.24). The current widening participation discourse, therefore, effectively steals the agenda for equal opportunities and silences other agendas on that topic.

This is not to deny the many positive features in the new reports. Many statements lead the education services on to a more open and flexible service. Kennedy, for instance, talks about 'bringing learning to learners wherever they are' (p.8) and 'at the right cost' (p.9) and of 'stimulating demand' (p.13) with 'targets for participation' (p.14). There is also much emphasis on encouraging local participation strategies - though without a delineation of what local participation might mean. These are constructive and proactive statements which raise the public profile of education and learning. There is an implicit assumption in them, however, that non-participants are in that situation through their own lack of interest. The danger behind these statements is that they fail to recognise the possibility that people may already be learning in their own way. Similarly, whilst uncertificated learning is acknowledged as an important step on the ladder to achievement of participation targets, it is not recognised as a goal in itself.

The Fryer report (1997) came after Dearing and Kennedy. It shifted those reports towards a more holistic view of learning. It talked, for example, about the implementation of lifelong learning through an enlarged range of modes of study but with more ownership over learning development by individuals and communities (p.35). It was the first report to mention older adults as learners, particularly in the broad context of active citizenship and good health (p.26). The report asked for more sophisticated measures of learning activity advocating new criteria and methods of data collection which reflect the 'diversity of forms and locales of lifelong learning' (p.37). In contrast to the Dearing report in particular, there is even recognition of the need for institutional change if new participation models are to be effective (p.46). The report's overall strategy appeared, however, to raise issues rather than suggest ways of implementing change. Its primary purpose was to pave the way for legislative measures.

In the event, the Government's response to all the above reports was a consultation document The Learning Age (DfEE 1998). This document tried to merge holistic images of learning with the aforementioned European drives towards developing a model of lifelong learning which is linked to skills updating and employability strategies. As such it revealed a political tension between the rhetoric of the Fryer Report and more instrumental commitments towards upskilling the British workforce. The Learning Age provided a definition of lifelong learning for example which emulates the European model as: 'The continuous development of the skills, knowledge

11

and understanding that are essential for employability and fulfilment' (p.11); whilst at the same time envisioning a society which values learning for its own sake. As stated earlier, this strategy in itself has two positive outcomes. Firstly learning is fore-fronted on the political agenda and new modes of learning are evident. This will make some forms of learning more accessible than they were. Many people in the past were simply not encouraged to continue learning in any formal or pro-active sense. The overall focus on the development of an employable workforce is, of course, desirable and essential for economic growth. There is even recognition that: 'Many people's life experiences and knowledge should entitle them to recognition and accreditation which they have not received in the past' (ibid: 47).

These issues are important. The danger, however, is that they are being seen in the context of dominant social patterns which already exclude those people who are not part of the immediate employability and 'normal' market. The rhetoric, in its eagerness to promote learning of all kinds, does little to define what counts as valuable learning, beyond that which is already accredited. There appear to be contradictions, for instance, between the language of an inclusive learning agenda and the practical suggestions therein. For example, one part of the document refers to qualifications for adults which should include a 'wide variety of skills and subject matter' (p.66). However, subject matter is not defined and the emerging boundaries for a nationalised National Qualifications Framework suggest something specific about 'flexibility'. Indeed much of the more general references to adult learning formats are understood as literacy and numeracy, with little or no recognition of plurality or diversity of individual goals for learning. These assumptions about learning extend to perspectives for higher education. For example, widening participation simply means: 'Anyone who has the capability for higher education should have the opportunity to benefit from it' (p.49). This, of course, implies that HE itself does not need to change. The goal of widening participation, then, is using strategies for inclusion which have only ever succeeded with the already included.

Schuller (1998), Oppenheim (1998) and Schuller and Burns (1999) suggest that one way forward is to broaden the economic view of education and training, as a form of investment in human capital, to include the concept of 'social capital'. Social capital is seen as the missing link between identifying social groups who participate in lifelong learning and those who do not. Proponents of social capital do not deny the need for human capital (skills development), but they suggest that a closer understanding of social capital will help us understand the broader social environments 'which foster lifelong learning' (Schuller & Burns 1999: 54).

12

Social capital is seen as a cumulative set of shared values, social networks, communication strategies and supportive environments. This could mean membership of clubs or aspects of community cohesion which foster an investment in collective, rather than individual self interests. Proponents of social capital claim that those who are more active citizens are also more active learners. It will be argued, however, that whilst concepts of social capital do have economic value for the lifelong learning agenda, the nature of what counts as valuable social networks is still culturally defined - with consequent effects on certain sectors of the population. There is already a dominant understanding of achievement or progression goals, for instance. Their value is for a particular kind of economy from which those in the third speed are often excluded by virtue of their absence from the labour market or other socially acceptable organisations.

In summary, the new discourse of education recognises the problem of exclusion, but in addressing this problem as a cohesive project, makes some of the issues which constitute the problem, invisible - for example the issue of structural unemployment, the issue of age, the fact that some people are only indirectly contributing to the labour market as an intermediary between generations. Other unrecognised issues relate specifically to the nature of institutional provision and what counts as worthwhile learning. These issues will become clearer as the following chapters start to question some of the assumptions that widening participation can be addressed by a linear and unproblematic strategy. The next chapter presents some theoretical arguments which reinforce my position that the dominant education world has adopted and internalised its practices in such a way that it unwittingly excludes even when it thinks it is being inclusive.

2   Who has authority to know?

The last chapter talked about the emerging political agenda for widening participation in post compulsory education. The renewed focus on continuing education suggests, implicitly at least, that it is a new concept for certain sectors of society. Such a position also implies that the knowledge gained by those certain sectors of society up to now has been invalid. It might perhaps be argued that the current emphasis on learning which privileges the skills of learning how to learn is simply replacing the hierarchical notion of 'knowledge' with a more level playing field notion of 'skills' (Edwards 1999). Nevertheless, the new learning politics fails to adequately address the question: What counts as worthwhile knowledge in a rapidly changing and fast moving society? Consequently (if there is a relationship between knowledge and learning) the current education agenda is not in a position to define what will count as acceptable learning for the future. The shifting boundaries of knowledge have been discussed elsewhere (Scott 1997, Barnett and Griffin 1997, for instance). The argument that people have different ways of knowing and formulating knowledge has also been raised, particularly amongst feminist writers (Code 1991, Hill Collins 1990, bel hooks 1994, Belenky et al 1986, Skeggs 1997). People have even cited the consequences of these arguments for the teaching process (Aronowitz and Giroux 1993, Usher, Bryant and Johnston 1997).

Nevertheless the question remains - if there are all these anomalies about knowledge and learning, why is some knowledge still regarded as authoritative and worthwhile and other knowledge not? One purpose of this study is to demonstrate how certain kinds of knowledge are simply disregarded because of who acquires them. Another purpose is to show how individuals internalise a belief that only some knowledge counts and only some people have authority to know. As a result individuals and those around them make decisions about learning and related matters based on perceived rationales about what is best or appropriate for them, rather than a real recognition of latent ability or even understanding about the value of what they already know. Then when some people - as many did in this study - try to resist their imposed learner identity, a number of other factors come into play which make such resistance difficult to realise. The resultant effect is a perception, by those with authority to know, that some

14

people simply do not want to learn. This perception in turn affects strategies for social inclusion. Such strategies often mean that people are told what to learn and why it is important for them to gain that particular kind of knowledge or understanding.

This chapter looks at how such situations arise. It provides a theoretical justification for challenging some unproblematic principles for adult and university education. It explains the book's attempt to question the unquestionable and pose the unthinkable. I shall talk about particular themes which crop up throughout the ensuing chapters. Together these themes enable me to explain why social exclusion persists in university continuing education. It also provides me with an opportunity to look for ways forward in addressing the problem. The themes cover notions of language, discourse, knowledge and power. They include an analysis of how history constructs partial views of past events. In other words I shall explain how social conditioning creates belief, behaviour and identity.

My principal argument is that social conditioning is brought about by different kinds of power relationships and dominant societal values. The dominant values enable the emergence of a hierarchy of informed wisdom (knowledge). Those values control the means by which knowledge and truth are determined. Similarly, people's interpretations of truth and their own sense of self depend on where they are positioned in society. However, as such situations are determined through the (usually unequal) balance of power in relationships, rather than fixed positions, I shall also argue that it is and has been possible for individuals to develop insights which enable them to question or move beyond the position that is expected of them. These tensions between expectation for, compliance with, internalisation of and resistance to certain ideas and values will become apparent throughout the individual stories and their critical life events. All these stories show there are many factors influencing who participates in education, especially higher education. They are explained primarily by using Foucault's understanding of power, discourse and knowledge.

Power, discourse and knowledge

Foucault provides one of the more elaborate definitions of power. Whilst his analysis is not everyone's cup of tea, it enabled me to understand and explain connections between institutional practices with regard to education and the apparent non participation of different socio economic groups. Foucault offers, for example, an explanation for shifting meanings and expectations for societal behaviour over time. He highlights discontinuity,

15

rather than continuity, of ideas which are commonly presented in the name of progress.

Power, for Foucault was seen as a relationship rather than the more tangible notion of power as an act or outcome. He saw power as something fluid - which happens between people - to which everyone has access and in which everyone plays a part. The interaction between two or more people, how they speak, behave and believe, is therefore one of power. The balance of power may be more or less equal. The way people speak or use language is one way of making visible the kind of power relationship in being at any given point in time. So also are behaviour patterns and so are institutional structures and other societal systems. For Foucault the latter are all some form of discourse - mechanisms of the power relationship. Some discourses are more dominant than others. The reproduction of dominant discourses creates the social structure and status quo in societies. These discourses and power balances in any relationship are usually held in place by the hierarchical status (official or not) of the participants in a given society. That is, some people use more powerful discourses. They have authority to know. They are agents of power (Foucault 1980). Most people are so embedded in their societal belief systems that they neither question the dominant values nor realise how much they themselves are naturalised into them. Certain aspects of their behaviour become entirely predictable and unquestioned in their own social circumstances. They are 'normalised'.

So, for example, a doctor will not only behave towards a patient in a certain way, but the patient will also behave towards the doctor in a reciprocal way. Their power relationship is reciprocal. Both collude in it and both use predictable discourses (behaviours, language etc). Their behaviour is normalised (Fairclough 1989, Foucault 1980). Such a relationship is, of course, fragile and open to resistance to the norm on either part. Consequently there are other, wider, societal power relationships in place which minimise the risk of resistance. So, if either person behaved unpredictably other discourses (behaviours, acts, arguments of reason) and 'agents' of power (people with designated status in the hospital, surgery or wherever) would move into being. Most people have already internalised such discourses and therefore behave 'appropriately'. They have absorbed self surveillance mechanisms (discourses of 'disciplinary power') into their natural behaviours. Furthermore, both parties usually accept the unequal relationship. The doctor has authority to know and define. His or her knowledge in that relationship is the most powerful one (although mutual interaction of course is required to facilitate a diagnosis of the patient's ailment). Only certain knowledge, therefore, is powerful and only those who have the balance of power in their favour are

16

able to produce authoritative statements which might change the current discourse.

A more macro use of power, knowledge and discourse can be seen where politics and economics come into play. One example of such intervention - to follow the medical analogy - can be observed in discourses for psychiatric care. The arguments for psychiatric care can be seen to have changed over the years where the dominant power holders perceive there is political or economic gain to do so. The reasons for changing such discourses, however, are always argued on behalf of the least powerful in the relationship, ensuring their collusion and participation in the new discourse. So where confinement of people with psychiatric problems was once regarded as the best strategy for the patient and for the good of society, it is now discredited through the new rationale that confinement is cruel to the patient. The economic gain from the new discourse of community based care results in a cheaper care service under the political rationale of 'patient benefit'. Later chapters will show how similar discourses of 'care' have served to keep some groups of people away from educational opportunities rather than enhance their chances of participation. The ability to change arguments like these relies on our understanding of how they are set up in the first place and how they function on a daily basis.

People's positions within power relationships are multiple, of course. They play different roles according to the social composition of the participants in any interaction. But the status quo is usually maintained, Foucault argues, because power is both productive and repressive. People may therefore contribute positively to power relations because they perceive some gain (real or imagined) in doing so:

> If power were never anything but repressive ... do you really think one would be brought to obey it? What makes power hold good ... is simply the fact that it doesn't only weigh on us as a force ... but that it traverses and produces ... it needs to be considered as a productive network (Foucault 1980: 119).

The way society operates often militates against the success of individual efforts to resist the dominant view of the time. Foucault sought to explain how people internalised and normalised their unchallenging behaviour or attitudes as a form of self regulation. He called this 'disciplinary power'. This is a means of self control where people survey their own behaviours as if they were being watched from an imagined, all-seeing gaze. By policing themselves in this way people are taking away their own will to resist by internalising as 'common sense' certain rules and norms. They become players in their own ideology: 'Discourses define what is normal and what

17

is normal is then seen as in need of normalisation or conformity to the norm' (Ramazanoglu 1993: 22). The subordinated then behave in a way that is expected of them by the dominant. The dominant, too, behave in a way that is expected of them.

Foucault described disciplinary power as a sophisticated and efficient, modern form of power which holds itself in place by a 'closely linked grid of disciplinary coercions' designed to solve the problem of surveillance (1980: 106). The linked grid would consist of institutional structures, conditions and hierarchies where individuals oversee each other:

> The interplay of the family, medicine ... the school and justice ... establishing connections, cross references ... and demarcations ... its a machine in which everyone is caught, those who exercise power just as much as those over whom it is exercised (Foucault 1980: 157-159).

The key principle of these coercions is the individual's internalisation of their own surveillance and its perceived normalisation process. People believe they must conform because they believe in the expectations of their conformity, so that the system is: 'taking away their wish to commit wrong ... mak[ing] people unable and unwilling to do so' (p.154). The origin of this idea lay in an 18th century physical invention by a man called Jeremy Bentham. The 'panopticon' was a watchhouse designed to control prisoners by the most efficient method possible. That is, one guard would retain a central position from which he could observe the behaviour of prisoners. As prisoners could not see the guard they did not know when they were being watched, so would behave at all times as if they were.

The potentially unpredictable combinations of power relations and discourse interactions (as the mechanisms for power relations) renders the possibility of resistant forms of discourse and the possibility of changing power relationships. Agents of power and their discourses are therefore constantly under threat - hence the intricate networks of agencies, institutions, discursive practices such as rules and internalised rationalities, for sustaining the status quo: 'Power is a persistent registration of truth' (Foucault 1980: 93).

Foucault saw education institutions as particularly sophisticated networks of disciplinary power. They possess carefully constructed discourses which ensure their authority to hierarchise knowledge and define how it is taught. Whilst some writers feel that position is changing, (Scott 1997, for example), the institutional infrastructure nevertheless maintains many ways of being which their inmates simply take as given. Such ways often pass unchallenged and unnoticed in the drive for reform. Indeed it would be unthinkable to change them. As Berger (1963) intimated, people's behaviour is naturalised so much that they are channelled into certain grooves of being. Those grooves appear to the individual the only possible ones. Bourdieu (1993) went even further to suggest that the discourses of education institutions - and higher education ones in particular - are ones of cultural capital - distinctive, naturalised ways of being and reasoning which give their inmates a working currency for domination or prestige. This is not to say that universities have not changed - especially in the past few years. But they have not changed from within. Rather the wider political and economic arguments are creating new rationales for change under the umbrella of vocationalism and wealth creation. The balance of power is being infiltrated but for different benefits than those perceived for the learners in this book. The nature and speed of external motivators for change, moreover, is always in constant tension with the power base from within.

Foucault identified five systems or modes of power for educational institutions. He suggested that the core values of all education institutions are sustained and reinforced by the same set of self-preserving, interdependent functions. These protect the institution's ethos and deflect deviant attempts to infiltrate new values, beliefs or forms of knowledge. This is his explanation for how power functions in education. The functions are simplified here but divide up briefly as follows:

- a system of 'differentiation' which gives particular status to individuals, as defined by their title in the institution
- a set of assumed behaviours - the roles which people enact upon each other, including how they teach or assess quality
- the written or unwritten rules of behaving - the self 'surveillance' of disciplinary power and ways in which procedures are followed by individuals or groups
- the institution's committee systems and management structures within which decisions are made
- the kind of rationalities which are used - the articulated arguments and meanings for why things are as they are, or should be done (from Foucault 1982: 222-223).

An application of these terms to university practice might be interpreted in this way. The systems of differentiation include the hierarchical status of professor, senior lecturer, clerical staff etc, with professors having most 'authority to know' a subject. The set of assumed behaviours refers to teaching roles, student roles and administration roles which assume a reciprocal relationship to each other. The rules of disciplinary power include, for example, the ways in which individuals follow procedures for setting up a new course or marking an essay. The university's committee systems are best exemplified by the structures for processing a new course proposal or degree structure. The institutional rationalities are those common sense arguments for higher education such as notions of level, authoritative texts, good research or excellence.

Chapter three in particular explores how such systems operated in one institution. Chapter four gives some indication of how those systems are replicated across universities, as well as showing examples of deviance (or resistance to the norm) and how that is dealt with by higher education.

The world is not quite so simple and well organised as this, of course. Many feminist writers argue, for instance, that people are not always trapped so neatly within their discourse. There are times when individuals may find their own sense of personal agency (self determination) which enables them to move beyond their immediate situation (Ransom 1993, Soper 1993). Individuals also acquire personal experiences and memories and attach individualised meaning to those memories. Whilst they may function within a certain dominant discourse, they experience different discourse interactions so each personal experience and understanding of themselves and their world is unique. The distance between an individual's sense of self and the dominant perspective depends on how much they fit into the dominant view of normality.

The exposition of marginalised experiences amongst under-represented groups is one way of showing the inadequacy of certain dominant rationales for explaining normality. Shared memories of 'how it was' for them can even expose the inadequacy of officially recorded events in history. Personal stories may therefore be the untold realities of a period in time - selected out by the dominant view of history. Chapter six reveals the complexity of some stories amongst the course participants who lived several marginalised realities in relation to their gender, class, disability or culture. So what may appear true for one society, may not be so for other social groups:

> Each society has its regime of truth, its general politics of truth: that is, the types of discourse which it accepts and makes function as true and false statements, the means by which each is sanctioned; the techniques and procedures accorded value in the acquisition of truth; the status of those who are charged with saying what counts as true (Foucault 1980: 131).

As social groups do not operate in tandem, however, this means that some regimes of truth are subsumed as subordinate to others. This book is about reinvesting in surbordinated truths and meanings.

To summarise the arguments so far then, knowledge, as described by Foucault, is an outcome of power investment. The application of power is political, so that only some knowledge becomes powerful and therefore possesses economic value. Dominant knowledge is not necessarily a universal truth, though it may be perceived as such, due to the power mechanisms (discourses) in place. The university's position of neutrality, described in chapter one, is therefore simply a strategic discourse to sustain the power of certain viewpoints - to serve the interest of its institutional members (primarily male, middle class, white and able bodied): 'The exercise of power creates knowledge and conversely knowledge constantly induces effects of power' (Foucault 1980: 52). Knowledge is sustained through experts who perform, say and do, based on their own agency status and internalised understanding of the world.

In spite of this position Foucault and other writers argue it is possible to unearth other forms of knowledge. This is the kind of knowledge which rarely receives political status. It is often subjugated and disregarded by those with authority to know. As such it is seldom identified in texts (Oliver 1990, Hill Collins 1990, Lynch & O'Riordan 1998). It is nevertheless a crucial plank in the reinvestment of subordinated truths and discourses.

Subjugated knowledge

Subjugated knowledge is, Foucault says, delegitimated knowledge, local and without agency authority:

> Local, discontinuous, disqualified, illegitimate knowledges against the claims of a unitary body of theory which would filter, hierarchise and order them in the name of some true knowledge (Foucault 1972: 83).

This kind of knowledge is, many argue, privileged to certain marginalised groups or members, usually derived from experience rather than scientific proof. There is no consensus of terminology for these forms of knowledge but they are commonly understood to relate to the perspectives of the marginalised - who have an experientially different view of the world from the dominant (Stanley and Wise 1993, Cain 1993, Code 1995, Preece 1998, 1999). Whilst not all experience can be classed as knowledge, the shared

21

views of certain sectors of society reveal understandings and insights which, if recognised, would contribute to a broader understanding of events and thinking generally (Skeggs 1997). The discourses (ways of doing, believing and understanding) of such knowledges are not necessarily in direct opposition to dominant values because relationships and interactions are multiple. All discourses are therefore to some extent tainted by each other. Nevertheless alternative, subjugated knowledges, are the potential power bases for resisting the dominant social order. As such they are threatening and rationalised out by those with authority to know. Chapters five and eight reveal the many ways in which subjugated knowledge can be a teaching tool as well as a source of empowerment for socially excluded groups if this knowledge is given public recognition. The consequence of such recognition can lead to an increased sense of self and more positive learner identity. Identities, however, are also complex and interlaced with functions of social capital. They are multiply influenced by their social environment. They are a critical feature of social exclusion as well as inclusion. A whole chapter (chapter nine) is devoted to discussing how the course participants acquired and developed their learner identities before and after the community courses. Foucault did not really explore identity in great depth. It is necessary to turn to feminist literature to explain more fully how identities are formed and reformed, particularly in relation to discourses. The term 'subjectivity' is often used to give a fuller understanding of identity and its context.

Identity (subjectivity)

Individuals build up an understanding of how they are expected to relate to others and how they are expected to behave through their exposure to certain discourses. Multiple identities form as a result of exposure to multiple discourses and over time a person builds up an accumulated sense of self. Subjectivity is a term used by poststructuralists to explain how the individual, as both a 'subject' (user) and 'object' (on the receiving end) of discourses, forms a view of his or her relationship to others. Weedon describes this as: 'The conscious and unconscious thoughts and emotions of the individual, her sense of self and her ways of understanding her relation to the world' (1987: 32). This self image is a consequence of power relations being played out alongside immersion in certain societal belief systems. Subjectivity becomes an internalised understanding of ourselves through our interface with the world around us (Rutherford 1990).

22

Like everything else in the interplay of discourse and power, subjectivities are not only multifaceted but they are also constantly changing. They are an outcome of different social constructions in the context of prevailing political climates. So, for example, the subjectivity of someone with cerebral palsy is constructed out of labels provided by professionals, friends and family. If those labels are primarily ones of inability, need, fragility, specialness and exclusion from the labour market then individual belief systems internalise those images as part of their sense of self. Chapters six and seven reveal the omnipresence of such discourses for some people. The consequence of internalised identities affects motivation, ambition, expectation for the self and others around us. Chapters eight and nine, however, reveal how even small experiences which diverted from the norm could empower individuals to construct new identities and change their understanding of themselves in relation to the wider world. The community courses in which I was involved were sometimes a catalyst for this change process. At other times critical life experiences could also provide similar stimuli. So 'subject positions' and identities are not fixed. They are constantly in progress and: 'acquire specific meanings in a given context' (Brah 1992: 143). As such, subjectivities are a product of society but also precarious and open to change. This interplay of identity, which has emerged from certain discourses, with the potential to alter, through the interweaving of new discourses, is a positive focus for this book. Learners and their self understanding in this study were sometimes constrained by a range of colluding discourses which disempowered them from achieving their potential. At other times their learner identities might be reconstituted through interfacing with new experiences. Those experiences altered the balance of power in their favour by giving the marginalised subject a voice and sense of personal agency.

This theoretical approach is characterised by an emphasis on fluidity, interconnections, shifting and dominating positions which screen out others. The stories of the adult learners and academics reflect these contradictions. But the position of the dominant discourses in higher education is challenged throughout this book in relation to all the other, normally screened out positions of the marginalised. The potential for resistance and change is evident, but without political and economically validated support such potential is rarely realised. Chapter one showed that the economic rationale for increased participation has already influenced political discourses. But the more fragile argument that the marginalised need their own voice within the new learning spaces being promoted has yet to be

23

won. This book hopes to move that argument forward and demonstrate the necessity for new discourses to effect real inclusion.

The remainder of this book uses the above ideas to explain and compare the relationship between community based learners and university concepts of appropriate university education. The next chapter starts with the university where I worked. It refers to the year of change-over to credit for LAE courses and compares how the LAE and community programmes described their various forms of education. It starts with an explanation of some of the tensions between two of the department's arms of provision - LAE and community. I use Foucault's theory of institutional power to show how those tensions were played out, including how they were represented in their academic review process.

3 That's not a university subject

The universities

> Social inclusion, like social exclusion, is becoming a politically attractive concept ... it diverts attention away from the possible need for radical change and encourages compliance with the status quo (Barry 1998: 5).

This and the following chapter look at the struggles within institutions to effect the kind of change which would include, rather than assimilate difference. In total 13 staff from four university continuing education departments contributed to discussions about higher education and community provision. They included a post 1960s, 'greenfields' university and two, older, 'civic' institutions. All the university profiles were characterised by a largely white, middle class population, though each hosted approximately 20% mature and 20% overseas students. The 'mainstream' of each university activity consisted primarily of three or four year degree programmes for full time students. All degree programmes would be validated by their subject department and then a faculty committee structure before receiving approval by the university's overall management strands, usually culminating in Senate approval. The discussion here concentrates on university departments with responsibility for adult and continuing education (CEDs). CEDs were non subject specific and organised around the needs of part-time adult students. Whilst each CED offered a range of provision from trade union partnerships to employer-based programmes my comments focus round two distinctive strands - short, award bearing, previously LAE courses and the community education version of that provision. The CEDs were grappling with the transfer of their short courses from non-award bearing to a part-time credit accumulation system and the accommodation of new validation processes which dealt with a wide range of subjects. Validation in CEDs needed to reflect sufficient subject (discipline) consultation across all relevant cognate departments. In addition each CED employed one or two academics to take responsibility for community education of the kind described in chapter one.

25

At the same time my university (university Z) was subject to its own departmental academic review and a costly restructuring exercise. These activities provided me with a rich source of records and inter-departmental correspondence with which to supplement my various face to face discussions across the universities. Though the events described in this chapter all occurred in my own (at the time) university department, chapter four includes comments from staff in the three other universities.

For my community programme the criteria for learner involvement was agreed in 1991. That is, learners must have academic qualifications of no more than their post 16 school leaver, GCSE equivalent. This boundary indicated the participants were unlikely to have previously considered higher education for themselves. These criteria alone gave the programme a label of difference - or deviance - within the department. As for the other universities, each responded to the needs of their local geography and demographics. But the programmes were broadly similar in their focus and client populations.

The roots of perceived tensions in higher education between notions of difference and quality, innovation and standards run deep. In university Z both the new continuing education (LAE) and its community education (CP) arm were caught up in these tensions on parallel levels. Correspondence within and to my own university department exemplified similar issues. The LAE staff, anxious to maintain a performance image which matched the values of mainstream departments, struggled to encompass the deviant CP programme which seemed to transgress all academic rules, even in a department which regarded itself as innovatory and flexible. Similarly, LAE struggles for academic autonomy as well as wider institutional acceptance weaved through all interactions across the university. Underlying these exchanges seemed to be a feeling by each party that the particular nature of their provision was misunderstood by the others, resulting in apparent avoidance of issues or lack of recognition of salient features.

Foucault's power systems, or modes, seemed to operate almost like a set of concentric circles. Each circle would attempt to fend off the perceived deviant circles furthest from its central, common sense values. The written correspondence which flowed from these circles added a very visible dimension to the way meanings were given to certain words. Fairclough (1995) calls this use of the written word 'genre' or 'text convention'. It gives the 'text' in documents its own normality within particular social contexts.

This chapter looks at some written attempts to defend or reply to 'difference', both in and outside the department. They show how difference is received within the institution and where its boundaries for difference lie. The wording in the text samples shows how some correspondence presumes superiority over, and marginalises, other documents which come across as deviant, simply because of the way they are written. The best place to start is with the department's academic review. This was an official report where I and the LAE team produced self-reflective reports to the review board of what we were doing. We were asked to write our reports under the following headings: introduction, programme objectives, nature of students and support systems, progression routes and modes of delivery. Even these headings broadly match Foucault's five institutional systems outlined in chapter two. 'Objectives' and 'modes of delivery' represent the institution's *set of assumed behaviours* while 'staffing' and 'nature of students' can loosely fit under the heading of *systems of differentiation. Rules of behaviour* refers to the review heading 'progression routes'. The 'introduction' frames Foucault's *kinds of rationalities*. The *committee structure* of the programmes is already embedded in the university's faculty and departmental procedures. Seen in this theoretical framework, the university's prescribed headings serve as powerful controlling mechanisms which survey and contain the institution's activities.

There is only space to look at a small section here, but the following extracts immediately indicate tensions of meaning between the two programmes. The LAE text (sample 1), for instance, included a number of phrases from the university's mission statement as validation of its ethos. The idea, of course, was for the LAE programme to be seen as acceptable to the wider university. The way it did so was through a form of self surveillance - a monitoring of its own behaviour. Firstly, any changes in practice were firmly attributed to the new political discourses of credit accumulation. They were 'as a result of the decision by HEFCE' (Higher Education Funding Council of England). Then the report ensured that the primary activities met institutional mission statements.

The review report was its own panopticon. It adopted university versions of knowledge and behaviours to describe a range of course provision. 'Flexibility', for example, meant part time study but not much else. Staff were listed according to their subject disciplines which aligned with those across the mainstream university, reinforcing its existing power-knowledge structures. The objectives assumed 'highly qualified', meant people with academic qualifications and that therefore 'highest quality' flowed from that position.

Text sample 1 - extracts from LAE review report, university z

Objectives

The [LAE] Programme seeks to support the Department's mission by:

- providing flexible certificate and short courses to meet a variety of learning needs
- encouraging access to the University by the widest possible range of students
- providing guidance to students in order to assist them in the development of their academic potential
- maintaining a pool of highly-qualified teaching staff, and sustaining and promoting the highest quality of teaching
- monitoring and evaluating courses to maintain and enhance the quality of its provision

... In addition to the existing Staff Tutors in Science, Humanities, Languages, Distance Learning and Intensive Courses, the Department needs full-time Staff Tutors in the areas of Creative Arts, Social Sciences and Health Studies ...

Nature of students and support systems

... the typical [LAE] student has changed ... Historically ... many were professional, or retired professional people, over the age of 55, who wished to study for interest. ... it is anticipated that future students will represent a younger age group, and may be seeking academic qualifications in support of personal or vocational goals.

... For students with a disability, we are able to offer

- initial discussion of requirements ...
- loan of portable and personal induction loop systems ...
- information and handouts in alternative formats ...
- information about disabled access ...
- free places for helpers ...

Educational guidance

... Students who require help in studying are encouraged, via the brochure and course tutors, to contact [LAE] ... [The department] has two educational guidance officers who can advise existing and potential students on the education programmes open to them.

Progression routes

... In order to facilitate progression the Department has promoted the following routes:

- Links with the Open College ...
- Certificates have a modular structure, which provides flexibility of entry and exit points...
- Different formats of provision to enable a wider choice of learning mode (pp 18-24).

28

Words like academic and quality would therefore ensure an unexplained position of acceptance and assumed set of shared values with the readers. In other words, as Fairclough (1989) stated, reflecting the sentiments of chapter two:

> Institutional practices which people draw upon without thinking often embody assumptions which directly or indirectly legitimise existing power relations. Practices which appear to be universal and common sense can often be shown to originate in the dominant class or the dominant bloc and to have become naturalised (p. 33).

Where differences did occur, they were well justified and contextualised within new political discourses. So the report's identified changing nature of continuing education students, associated with the imposed credit system, was supported by a new rationale for study around notions of 'personal growth' and 'vocational development', the vocabulary of Government policy. Similarly explanations of 'progression' and 'formats of delivery' were linked to linear and acceptable credit routes. Later in the report course development was rationalised under the academically acceptable notion of:

> collaboration with other university departments ... Collaboration usually involves working directly with an individual member of staff from another department, with the consent of the Head of that Department (p.24).

Such connections of meaning, however, were harder to apply for the community programme (CP). Indeed the document's main editor, found my section hard to accommodate within the whole document, stating that: 'its style is very different'. Perhaps some indicators of its difference can be discerned from my use of vocabulary and the way I presented its argument under the prescribed review headings.

As I began to write my report, it became necessary to re-define, and therefore explain at greater length, the guideline headings for CP. For instance, in its first paragraph I aligned the programme with its own version of values which lie outside the cultural capital of higher education. The programme was introduced as 'equal opportunities driven' and for: 'people who would not normally consider entering higher education or adult education'- as opposed to the 'non standard students' phraseology of the university's central planning statement. Such people, so described in the report, are not identifiable in the normative cohort of university students. The description 'not normally consider' runs counter to the notion of an adult learner as self-directed and sits uneasily with the perception of higher education as a goal to be reached through highly motivated personal study.

Text sample 2 - extracts from community review report

The Community Programme develops its courses directly for identified learner groups through ongoing consultation with a variety of non-specialist agencies, non-traditional students and curriculum areas. ... to attract new learners into liberal adult education for social or community development ...

Objectives:

- demonstrate the potential for new learner involvement in HE ... with learning support which is appropriate to the practical, cultural and personal needs of participants
- develop this provision in collaboration with partners drawn from community agencies and colleges across the region ...
- evaluate all activities; to relate them to research and publications which in turn will inform future practice
- maintain a national profile in relation to all of the above.

... Staffing the Community Programme poses a number of challenges:

- the need to provide role-model staffing
- the need to provide staffing with appropriate community liaison experience, an understanding of the learning needs of non traditional students and an understanding of higher education expectations
- the need to provide locally based staff who understand the needs and contacts in their local area...

Tutors are usually selected for their role model status and/or understanding of the group's background after confirmation of their teaching abilities.

Nature of students and support systems

Under-represented groups currently fall within two or more of the following categories:

- long term unemployed
- recovering from mental health problems
- of minority ethnic origin
- having a physical disability
- having young children or other care dependants
- in low socio-economic circumstances
- having left school with few or no qualifications
- studying for the first time at retirement age.

... The above student groups are usually taught in familiar surroundings amongst people they know and trust ...Support systems are drawn from the community in which the groups meet or live: they consist of culturally aware, role model personnel, a range of educational guidance, and practical support needs such as transport, childcare, flexible timetabling, translators, computers etc (pp 25-28).

Indeed the word student was often substituted throughout this section by 'learner', denoting a different type of educational relationship which is based round values of life-based learning, rather than the usual expectations for academic study. Community participants, then, are potential deviants for the university, threatening its values and expectations for student behaviour.

Collaboration for this programme, unlike the LAE section, did not mean intra-university (subject-specialist) collaboration, but: 'with a variety of non-specialist agencies'. Staffing members were not, as they were for LAE, recruited on the basis of subject specialisms, but for their 'role model status' and 'understanding of learner needs'. Staffing quality, then, is associated with experience and relationships, rather than possession of abstract knowledge, exemplified with PhD status.

Learning support was dissimilar to the LAE section in that it emphasised 'cultural awareness' and a range of tailor made support needs, as opposed to LAE's more tangible system of centrally provided equipment. The CP words placed too much emphasis on notions of fragmentation and difference - meanings which are difficult to inculcate into higher education learning values which derive from 'a common culture' (Robbins 1963).

A key objective in the CP report was to: 'demonstrate the potential for new learner involvement in higher education'. This statement re-directs provider motives away from an assumed, static service to a pro-active, exploratory mode where delivery and entry boundaries are blurred and malleable. It is harder for the higher education institution to support these objectives on the basis of excellence or high quality because they lie outside existing higher education boundaries of meaning. The university's powers of surveillance are further threatened by the report's non higher education funding criteria for performance, such as 'cultural relevance' (p.28). Indeed, the review panel asked for an explanation of cultural relevance, while 'quality' as a descriptor for LAE, went unchallenged throughout the review process.

CP's concept of cultural relevance stirred up contentions throughout the year within the department. For the university, all its courses are culturally relevant because the academic culture recognises courses within the provider's stated subject disciplines. Cultural relevance for CP meant of particular relevance to the learner, rather than the provider. Cultural relevance, therefore, would change according to the student group and their cultural background or socio economic experiences. Courses with cultural relevance for the learner meant acknowledging alternative, sometimes experiential, knowledges and perspectives. Institutional discourses already claim a position of neutrality, and only recognise knowledge as defined by

31

their own dominant cultural group through scholarship. Different cultural relevances were confusing and made no connection with existing academic parameters. Yet cultural relevance is a crucial feature of CP's notion of quality (Preece & Bokhari 1996, Preece 1999a); and a critical concern of marginalised cultures (Belenky et al 1986, Oliver 1990, hooks 1994).

Such mismatches of terminology occurred throughout the report. The headings 'educational guidance' and 'progression' provided evidence of two further differences in meaning. For the LAE report reference to educational guidance officers indicated a given role which was based on an expectation of student self direction:

> Students who require help in study are encouraged to contact Open Studies ...the Department of Continuing Education has two educational guidance officers who can advise students on the educational programmes open to them (p.21).

Educational guidance for CP was described, in a later section of its report, according to the holistic needs of adults rather than a responsive, one-to-one service to inquirers:

> **Educational guidance** plays an important role in the student support systems of the Community Programme. A number of methods are now taking place, including:
> - guidance as a group learning activity, integrated with course provision
> - mainstream guidance staff as a direct outreach support service to community groups
> - guidance as ongoing learner support to on-site students
> - the role of community staff, co-ordinators and tutors as guidance and learner support for community based learners
> - educational guidance as a filtering/access point for enquirers who are not ready for degree level study (p.28).

Equally 'progression' as a term was not questioned, beyond the identification of various linear 'routes' open to students on LAE courses. In the CP a new meaning and justification for progression had to be found. The CP text stated:

> Progression has been difficult to define for many participants ... research evidence of adult learner progression indicates that it is non-linear and not necessarily driven by qualifications. ... Progression for such students needs to be defined according to how they see themselves and also how support networks are able to assess their progress (p.28).

Compared with the LAE documentation this programme seemed much more fluid and intangible, in spite of its attempt to ground itself within the institution's rules by reference to research evidence.

In similar fashion CP's text exposition of the nature of learning needs, credit system and curriculum frequently required detailed explanation of content, in ways that were not necessary for the more discipline-centred LAE providers:

> The Foundation Credit scheme accredits skills acquisition ... each course has a generic skills curriculum yet can be adapted to include particular topic areas. Tutors are employed to teach at a range of levels according to the learning needs of students ... teaching requires careful attention to the mismatch between literacy levels ... cognitive ability, experience and understanding of the subject matter ... such work would not be possible within a standard accreditation scheme (p.30).

I might argue that such experiences outlined for CP have wider quality implications for both curriculum and teaching excellence across the post compulsory system. Yet the LAE report implied a perception of the student as a homogeneous, motivated adult learner - who may at most require study skills support or, perhaps, disability learning aids. Its language did not incorporate CP's detailed explication of student learning levels or additional needs. The higher education power-knowledge base does not require recognition of such differences. Such positioning of 'the subject' (learner) is superfluous to definitions of quality. CP was therefore simply seen as a form of resistance. As a result its criteria for quality and value were often neutralised, disempowered and marginalised - unrecognised in the university's notion of educational normality. The Review Panel Final Report, for instance, questioned whether CP's activities were 'appropriate for a university'.

The documents from both programmes explained their respective styles, practices and objectives. Their different uses of the same vocabulary and associated meanings demonstrate how the institution has a power relationship over normality and knowledge. The discourses within the institution normalise certain ways of viewing higher education. Their agents (the academics) sustain certain meanings as normal and therefore powerful. This is done through actions designed to ensure certain objectives are carried out in accordance with institutional values.

In spite of this, the CP objectives pursued their own power relationship with community learners. This indicates the potential for resistance within power systems. The effectiveness of that resistance is constrained, however, in a small corner of the institution. So, although CP's text demonstrates resistance through its own stated objectives, there are other layers of power managed by those with designated authority to undermine such moves, especially when the institutional core or its wider surveillance systems are threatened. Foucault's 'systems of rationalisation' show how institutions protect and legitimise their activities. One such incident happened some months before the academic review took place.

The legitimising of current practice

> Rules for social conduct are inherited from the past and constrain as well as facilitate behaviour. ... they may be compatible one with another as part of a relatively unified system, or there may be inconsistencies and contradictions between them (Allen & Macey 1998: 112).

It occurred at a departmental committee which was processing LAE courses for approval. The meeting took place shortly after two race awareness events in the department and a commitment to address race inequalities in staffing and curriculum development. I commented at the committee meeting on a course which I felt was not addressing these issues adequately. Its title was 'Black women and the Blues', and was due to be taught by a white man.

At the teaching committee I said that the race of the tutor meant that the course would not offer a black perspective; nor did the bibliography include writing from black people. I stated that black people would not attend such courses run by white people, in spite of the apparent syllabus relevance. Subsequent dialogues lasted several days. The following statements were offered various staff in defence of their proposals. I listed them in this format for a subsequent meeting:

Text sample 3a

1) The blues curriculum on offer is really about: America, about Music (in spite of its syllabus headings of: 'black feminism', 'black women's oppression in the South', 'history of slavery for black women in the South').
2) Black issues and courses and participants are really the community programme's responsibility.
3) Nobody has time to find new tutors, recruit new audiences.

4) It is too expensive to recruit role model tutors who may have to be brought in from further afield.
5) The audience will be white anyway, so who is going to notice the black issue.
6) The tutor is a known local expert in Blues music and academically acceptable.

My response at the time, in the subsequent meeting, was documented as follows:

Text sample 3b

1) The real curriculum is identified in the syllabus - what curriculum isn't delivered through art/ music/ literature/ history/ religion/ sociology/ psychology etc.? On this basis, there is no such thing as a multicultural curriculum.
2) To claim that only community courses should do non-white-based curricula isolates that programme as a marginalised provider with nothing to offer the mainstream, and with no access route into the mainstream.
3) By not recognising the need to recruit black staff as 'irrelevant' or 'unnecessary' or 'too difficult' denies the black voice, maintains the status quo and discriminates against black people who are effectively not acknowledged for their own distinctive contribution to cultural and race awareness or knowledge.
4) Such decisions deny our credibility for a commitment to raising the profile of black expertise, black tutors etc.

At the time I made two telephone enquiries concerning potential black tutors for the blues course. After the second telephone call I was able to supply the name of a local black woman tutor who had the qualifications to teach the blues course.

The result of these discussions was a decision that the tutor was already contracted to do the course but people's awareness had been raised for the future. The course's advertised title was changed to 'women and the blues' though the syllabus remained the same. In subsequent years the department did employ an African tutor to teach an African perspective course. Follow up equal opportunities meetings that year, however, did not result in either an agreed mission statement or code of practice.

This exchange highlighted for me the peculiarity of higher education talk which claims neutrality as a means of legitimising its practices. It confirms Foucault's theory that knowledge itself can become an authoritative medium of power which excludes difference and prevents change. It demonstrated his notion that there is an interconnecting network of power for sustaining dominant discourses: 'a total structure of actions brought to bear upon possible outcomes' (1982: 220). This particular set of LAE arguments was based on their internalised assumptions about expertise and subject discipline status which had long since passed critical scrutiny. Whilst the syllabus words positioned the course in the domain of black feminism, the meaning behind these words was reinscribed by the committee with a perception that the course was simply a music course - even though not one reference was made to musical composition, rhythm, stanza or any other academically identifiable music term. Similarly the removal of the word 'black' from the course title assumed a removal of the potential equal opportunities discrepancies in the course because the curriculum had already been reinterpreted. The expectation of a shared understanding within the institution justified their maintaining the status quo. This understanding assumed its own power to disguise the very existence of the language on the page. My resistance was positioned outside the university boundaries of reason - the cultural capital of universal 'neutrality' - and my knowledge claims at this point in time were interpreted as partial and deviant.

The problem of deviance was not confined to CP, however. LAE experienced similar struggles. The best exemplars of this came from individuals in cognate subject departments who were supporting, or not, new course proposals. To refer again to Foucault's network of institutional modes the following letter is argued on the basis of the writer's 'system of differentiation' - his pedagogic status to know.

The authority to decide what is an appropriate university subject

For the traditional university the curriculum was presented as the outward expression of accumulated private worlds of academic knowledge, mediated and given coherence by subject groupings and departments (Bocock & Watson 1994: 3).

The LAE programme had already, in anticipation of other departmental resistances to its activities, set its own disciplinary power procedures (self surveillance) in place, demonstrating a desire to conform to the dominant discourse of 'standards'. Firstly tutors for courses would be interviewed in the department and references taken up. Secondly course proposals would be forwarded to cognate departments for their comment and with a request for an internal assessor (moderator) for each certificate level course. Standardised letters, inviting comment, were written to relevant subject department academics. Sample 4 provides extracts from one such response to that invitation. It demonstrates the power of academic authority to define how 'socially situated' text can convey particular meanings (Fairclough 1992: 47). The academic was a historian replying to a plan by LAE to set up a credit bearing module called Family History.

Text Sample 4 - letter extract from cognate department

> I'm afraid this is a difficult proposal and one which I do not feel able to support. It raises several issues:
> 1)   Subject matter. I have always taken the view that courses on family history are not appropriate to university continuing education provision. It is essentially a nuts and bolts subject with only very limited academic content ... I have myself run courses with a family history slant ... but these were either courses on advanced techniques [example] .. or courses which tried to lead students from their interest in family history towards a wider interest in local history or social history. Given the very basic, source and technique related syllabus ... I do not think that this course is appropriate, certainly not as a credit bearing course.
> 2)   Tutor's background. It must surely be only in the most exceptional circumstances that a tutor without an education to degree level should be employed to teach a university course. ... I am sorry that my response is so negative but I simply do not believe that either course or tutor are appropriate to be included in the university's provision.

The letter uses academic argument from a self-sustaining, intrinsically logical and dispassionate standpoint. Phrases such as 'this is a difficult proposal' and 'raise several issues' place the letter in a context which implies refusal on grounds of reasoned argument and critical thought - the hallmarks of university superiority.

The remainder of the letter offers a series of rationales which frame the power-knowledge base for higher education. It assumes a shared understanding of 'appropriate .. level' and 'limited academic content'. The writer even gives examples of his boundaries for academic acceptability. The subject is one of 'nuts and bolts' with a 'very basic source and technique related syllabus'. Similarly the tutor cannot claim a qualification 'to degree level' in the subject. The writer's text, at first sight seems to have won its own argument. Yet all the arguments assume an unexaminable status behind both the tutor's expertise and the syllabus content. Without degree status, entry into the world of university teaching is barred. Critical analysis and teaching ability are inextricably linked to one descriptor - a degree qualification (even though the level of teaching required is only year one of an undergraduate course). Similarly, the wording of the syllabus is assumed to be the only indicator of what will actually occur in the classroom. The notion of learning as an experience for itself which stimulates wider interests, is unrecognised within academic criteria. The perceived meaning behind the syllabus words has placed this course outside the boundaries for university education. It is particularly interesting that the writer, in defence of his argument, admits to the value of this subject matter in a wider learning context, but only when embraced by a discursive practice with which he is himself familiar and which he is managing. (Indeed, later in this book this lecturer's expansion on the above point will be compared with the experiences of just such a course amongst one group of CP students).

The word 'appropriate' has appeared several times in this chapter. Fairclough (1992a) discusses at length the particular power value of 'appropriateness' as a concept. He discusses its use in national curriculum guidelines for schools where the guidelines stipulate that standard English is the appropriate means of communication. Appropriateness therefore assumes normativeness and consequently debases 'otherness'. Appropriate becomes normatively self defining, is prescriptive and signifies correctness. The significance of this word is that it helps: 'endow prescriptivism with a relatively acceptable face' (p. 37).

In academia, then, cultural capital has the power to protect itself as universal and common sense (Fairclough 1989). Rules and pedagogic status are reinforced through replicable control strategies and internalised behaviours which act as key power mechanisms for maintaining rationales and ensuring boundaries for appropriateness. When one system seems not to be effective, there are plenty of additional power techniques - through surveillance, agents, management structures, normative behaviours and rationalities. Discourse struggles and sites of resistance are ultimately lost in the prevailing cultural capital of value-free reason.

This chapter has used academic correspondence to show how certain discourses claim superiority and marginalise other discourses in one university department. If we accept the argument that all institutions operate in similar fashion:

> The tribes of academe ... define their own identities and defend their own patches of intellectual ground by employing a variety of devices geared to the exclusion of illegal immigrants (Becher 1989: 24).

Then it can only be assumed that other education institutions are performing similar exclusionary strategies without realising that they are doing so. To check this out I talked to academics in similar adult education departments in three other universities. LAE academics and CP staff told similar stories of two contrasting kinds of provision - that provided for the mainstream university participant and that provided for the community learner. The next chapter looks at how their stories interfaced with each other in their own institutions.

4 'We don't really belong'

Introduction

> Exclusion and inclusion as well as power, are closely linked to what goes on in education institutions: neither what is taught, nor who studies what, are neutral issues (Deem 1996: 51).

Chapter three showed how members of one university had a way of using certain words like 'appropriate', 'level', 'quality' and 'proper' without ever explaining what these words mean. There seems, therefore, to be an assumed common sense position that university work is quite simply 'excellent' and in need of no scrutiny. When outsiders offer alternative versions of excellence academics feel the need to defend, rather than alter, their position. This view was not confined to my own department, however, as the following discussions showed.

I talked to four department heads (HODs) and three established providers (LAs) of continuing education courses across the four different universities. I also talked to six people (CAs) who had specific responsibility for 'outreach' work in their local communities. From the outset there were differences in the starting points of these academics. Perhaps significantly the CAs had all entered higher education from an external post. Most of the mainstream academics (all the HODs and one LA) had spent their entire working career in higher education and they were all male. Everyone expressed a commitment to widening participation. Their perspectives differed, however, on how the institution should enable that process. Most of the discussions took place during the year when non award bearing courses were transferring to credit status. As a result all accredited, liberal courses are now subject to quality assurance systems which look like the procedures of other academic departments. I asked them all the same questions about quality, level, critical analysis, teaching and progression. Sometimes they were invited to clarify or pursue a particular point they had raised.

With a few exceptions, most of the HODs and LAs seemed caught in the same institutional power web that was outlined in chapters two and three. That is, arguments on behalf of higher education drew on the speaker's academic status 'to know' while 'surveillance strategies' in each institution followed almost identical committee procedures and rationalisations for

40

maintaining the status quo. Similarly, curriculum rules were never questioned. The CA staff, however, felt that rigid adherence to these rules was problematic for their participants. It restricted, for instance, interpretations of quality and valuable knowledge. The first section of this chapter gives some examples of more mainstream institutional positions and their self protective measures. The second section looks at alternative perspectives, provided mainly, though not exclusively, by the CA staff.

Who has authority to know?

The community staff occupied a peculiar position where they often had autonomy without authoritative status. CA2, for example, worked on externally funded projects which did not require committee approval because the courses were not accredited:

> I tend to work quite independently ... I make decisions for myself about how much I spend on something within a given budget ... so I've managed not to get caught into those sort of [committee] processes.

This relative autonomy would disappear once community staff tried to mainstream their work. CA3 cited one example:

> A pro-vice chancellor had a look at [accreditation of prior learning proposal] and said; 'never in my lifetime ... who is this CA3?' and you sort of feel about this high ... I think we feel we are both outsiders and we don't really belong.

Nearly all the community staff felt they were outsiders in their own institution. CA3 had been working at the university for approximately four years. Yet she and others in her position described themselves as having little authority. Consequently what she said also seemed to have little worth in the broader scheme of things.

In contrast, department heads were able to speak from a power base of 'director of continuing education' with authority to know - in particular what might be acceptable for course development. Both HOD3 and HOD2, for instance, identified times when they exercised that authority: 'There is a course that has been proposed called 'Starting Art' which was not an appropriate title' (HOD3); 'I've turned down course titles, everyone in the department knows I will never allow a course title to contain the word "fun"' (HOD2).

It will be seen in the second section that community courses were developed under very different criteria from their mainstream counterparts. In order to be clear about these differences I tried to find out what were the main continuing education rationales and mechanisms for ensuring course quality in higher education.

Strategies for maintaining institutional quality

The following quality assurance process was typical for accredited, as opposed to non award bearing, community courses:

> We have got the social science team, that is the first step ... then there is the department meeting; then there is the department board ... then there is the faculty undergraduate committee; then there is the faculty board; then there is the university standards, so really it is incredibly heavy (CA1).

The process only really seemed useful to those who had authority to influence the system. However, they were the least likely to want change. HOD3, for instance, felt this procedure required no explanation or amendment:

> I: What do you find unsatisfactory about the approval procedure?
> HOD3: I'm not sure if I find anything - it would be nice to know what CA3 said - anything especially unsatisfactory ...

CA3's unprompted reaction to the course approval procedure was: 'I feel I am hitting my head against a brick wall sometimes'.

When asked what precisely the committee members were looking for, HOD1 offered this explanation:

> We are looking for consistency of quality and consistency of assessment ... that people can form adequate reading and other course related material which they won't be able to judge emotionally because people are from cognate disciplines.

The distinction between unemotional and emotional perspectives was never explained. The question of alleged value-neutrality in HE curricula and the conviction that objects of knowledge are separate from knowers (Code 1991: 32-3) is a much debated issue amongst feminist writers. Certain

42

language is often associated with male ways of knowing and, therefore, the correct, unemotional way:

> Speaking with the authority of their institutional position masks the identity - indeed the existence of the cognitive agents whose values, in effect, shape and guide the inquiry. The facts, allegedly speak for themselves, the values on which they are based are suppressed (ibid: 35).

Other issues of quality, however, were not subject to such clear cut distinctions. The university's elaborate checking process, which might pick on words like 'fun', paid less attention to equal opportunities issues - as the last chapter also showed. Department heads and community staff were asked if their department had an equal opportunities policy. With the exception of one department, there was a discrepancy between the department head's opinion and that of his community staff. The following exchanges from one department are typical:

> I: does this department have an equal opportunities policy?
> CA3: No we don't. The university has but we don't ... I've been pushing him on us developing our own since I came here; rubbish, it really is.

The department head (HOD3's) response to the question compared with that of most heads and LA staff:

> I think we do. The institution as a whole has an equal opportunities policy. We have a mission statement, which that dimension of our work is based around some notion of equal opportunities and also some notion of how to address that.

The point of referring to these equal opportunities exchanges is their contrasting position to institutional notions of quality. Equality is not a requisite of quality. Indeed its importance is so fragile that the head would not necessarily know if their own department even had a formal policy. HOD2's commentary on a recent equal opportunities event for instance, confirms the peripheral importance of equal opportunities issues in higher education:

> We had a seminar on language and equal opportunities the other day which caused a really hilarious amount of resistance ... it was very good natured, not a problem.

43

Resistance presented as 'good natured' means the issue can also be minimised and therefore not enacted upon. It is unlikely, for instance, that 'critical analysis' would be viewed in the same way.

These examples are not rehearsed here with malicious intent. They simply demonstrate that the university institution does not criticise itself (Delamont 1996) and that equal opportunities issues are interpreted particularly loosely in higher education (Weiner 1998). Its boundaries already contain what is excellent and exclude what is not. Common sense understandings about what is appropriate are so internalised that they have moved 'beyond ideology' (Fairclough 1989). In Foucault's terms they are discourses. Behaviours, practices, beliefs and rationalities are all manifestations of the power relationship between authorised personnel and their identification of acceptable knowledge. The system is protected by quality assurance procedures designed to maintain the status quo, rather than to act as a self critical, reflective process. Committees are a form of social control, rather than a means of stimulating innovation or change. Discourse positions do change, of course, and the drive for credit in a previously non award bearing sector is one example. But they have changed largely by moving an existing menu of discourses round, rather like a kaleidoscope.

The teaching process, as another part of the institution's interlocking web of power, would serve to reinforce these positions.

How to teach in higher education

Perhaps the most intrenchable example of higher education's version of knowledge is its dependence on (academically authorised) text as <u>the</u> teaching medium:

> The essential style for somebody like me with a subject like mine is a seminar where everybody has read the text and they've all got the text in front of them and we look at the text and its a heavily textual analytical based seminar, out of which in the classic way larger ideas emerge and ... we're all taking notes (HOD2).

Although HOD2 suggested this style related to his own subject area, each liberal academic in turn produced a similar description, using text as the basis for developing further understanding. In fact when I tried to challenge this strategy LA2 responded:

44

> Well you've got to have something to engage with critically and since we've always tended to use the written word, it's difficult ... what are they operating with if there isn't any text?

I shall return to the relationship between text and knowledge later. But there were other aspects of academic study which proved equally intransigent. The reference to critical analysis was a case in point.

Critical analysis is generally regarded as central to higher education learning (Barnett 1988, 1990, 1997, for example). All the academics agreed on this point and liberal adult education perspectives are rehearsed in chapter one. Nevertheless the liberal interpretation (as opposed to the community version) of critical analysis was still bound by notions of text, neutrality and disciplinary knowledge: 'It's sort of probing behind what the author is saying' (LA2). HOD2, for instance stated:

> Universities are non-sectarian and non this and non that, they're supposed to be disinterested platforms on which you can approach any subject in the knowledge that it will be looked at with this cool eye of, yes, critical analysis. Nobody's going to be pushing any party lines in the university, that's the argument (HOD2).

The trouble with HOD2's apparently benign position is that 'any subject' would be interpreted quite specifically. Similarly 'non-sectarian' meant that everything would be analysed from the university's own unchallengable centre stage position. Everything would be judged against that norm, including what was an acceptable course or subject to study. HOD2 even extended this perspective to what was an acceptable teacher:

> If you ask a university what makes them excellent they'll say well it's easy you look at the CV of the person teaching it, are they academically our sort, have they got a PhD.

Of course, those who are 'academically our sort' are people who make up the majority of the university teaching profession - that is white, middle class, male (Halsey 1992) and able-bodied. Inevitably, selecting tutors who are 'academically our sort' means choosing more of the same. The implied neutrality of a position which sits in opposition to another viewpoint seems to have reproduced itself through several generations of the university's assumed authority to know. Only a combination of middle class values and university subject based material, supported by a PhD, counts as 'value free' and 'excellent'. Quality was therefore defined and maintained by the institution's own internalised code of excellence. Aspects which appeared to lie outside those values were simply not excellent. Even though some academics acknowledged the anomalies, the system's self surveillance mechanisms, and inherent understanding about itself, protected the status quo:

> It's about fitting in and if you do something that is particularly zany or off track then they have little mechanisms for making you come back in again (CA3);

> The university is looking over our shoulder and when it gets too innovative then they say, well hold on a minute, this is something you can't do (CA1).

An example of how academics seem unable to hear or see alternative perspectives came from LA1. Chapter three has already noted his refusal to allow the certification of a family history course at university level. Prior to that written exchange with the continuing education department, I invited him to explain why family history could not be considered a university course:

> Well I don't think that genealogy is really a university subject ... because in terms of history it is not actually encouraging so much of a questioning, it's encouraging people to actually gather facts without really questioning them and I would draw a distinction between that and I suppose family history in a slightly broader sense in terms of if you like the history of the family or the history of experiences of different families and we would see it as a way into social history ... rather than see it as an end in itself.

In its own way, this argument carries the same irrefutable logic as LA1's written correspondence. However it is the underlying relationship between him - the one with authority to know - and myself which reveals again Foucault's link between power and knowledge. Firstly LA1 reinterpreted my term 'family history' as 'genealogy'. He then described genealogy as being outside of the critical, questioning hallmark of higher education learning. He assumed my reference to family history would mean something less than his own. He then re-described his own version of family history as something different from that assumed to be practised in my community courses. In Foucault's terms this new description was the power-knowledge expression of his own authority. This incident will be compared, in chapter eight, to the community groups' descriptions of their own learning experiences.

Barnett (1997) has attempted to develop the notion of critical thinking to move it beyond this focus on specific disciplines. He describes the concept of 'critical being' as more emancipatory than traditional forms of critical analysis. His choice of development, however has been through interdisciplinary knowledge. This still limits critical analysis opportunities to the established authority of university knowledge bases:

> Interdisciplinarity is necessarily critical interdisciplinarity. It encourages the possibility of different cognitive perspectives being turned on a subject and so illuminating it in different ways (p.19).

Critical analysis therefore is associated with subject specific disciplines, confined to authorised scholarship, perceived through written texts. Barnett's attempt to move away from the incestuousness of intra-disciplinary critiques, merely succeeds in shifting perspectives around, but still within, higher education's cultural capital enclave. In Cherryholmes' (1988) words, then, the curriculum base barely changes in terms of acknowledging different voices:

> What students have an opportunity to learn refers to legitimate and approved communications and actions. What students do not have an opportunity to learn are those things off-limits (p.133) ... For example, do we want to provide opportunities to learn a structure of the disciplines at the expense of teaching about the causes and consequences of racism, sexism and social inequality and injustice (p.143)?

The issue of what counts as an acceptable argument, knowledge or valuable learning is central to the theme of social exclusion in this book. Whilst some of the senior and liberal academics felt the higher education system appeared to be accepting the idea of new students, few explored the implications of this in terms of knowledge creation or the student experience. I will argue later that recognition of different forms of knowledge on community courses would not easily translate into higher education's disciplinarity approach to learning.

The above extracts have highlighted some of the most unshifting values about university study. It is interesting to note the academics' occasional references, in their exchanges, to the word 'university' or 'institution', almost as a human form. This somehow deflected individual responsibility for university rules, thereby making the rules even more difficult to alter. In Foucault's language, the institution as a whole was its own panopticon for 'disciplinary power'. In other words, the university inmates engaged in an unconscious desire to behave under the watchful gaze of institutional rules and committee systems. In this context it is not surprising to find that the

47

community academics' definitions of quality were often regarded as deviant.

To demonstrate these deviant behaviours the next section refers primarily to comments from community staff as they struggled to reconcile their own, between-culture position. They talked about quality assurance measures, teaching styles and use of critical thinking in ways which were meaningful to their respective participants.

Academics talking differently

The community academics had a completely different way of describing how they taught and how critical thinking contributed to knowledge creation. They also had a different rationale for providing courses in the first place:

> I don't want to parachute into these communities and say this is what you've got to do for us to say you are doing anything of value ... I am not particularly interested in developing courses that fulfil a criteria that is not placed on it by the participants (CA2).

The development of community based courses often contrasts with the credit bearing model which assumes a variety of disinterested academics will scrutinise the syllabus words extraneously from their participants. CA2 described her own elaborate quality assurance activities. They were labour intensive and directly connected to the participants through an ongoing monitoring process:

> I would obviously talk to people about what they are going to do and make sure I feel it is an appropriate curriculum and part way through the course we will discuss that again. I also make a visit to each of the courses where I talk to participants and the tutor as a group.

'Appropriate' in this process was a very different interpretation from the 'unemotional' criteria outlined in the first section. I offered my own explanation of what an appropriate curriculum for an assertiveness course might look like for one community group:

> We talked to the Asian community centre about what kind of curriculum should be put into that course; we found an Asian tutor who had been on an assertiveness training course and she looked at the curriculum, decided which

48

bits would offend and which bits wouldn't offend and also got herself examples that would be relevant to the women's experiences.

The idea of 'value' for the community courses linked directly to what was valuable for the learner, but in a curriculum framework which encouraged analysis round relevant topics. Alongside these exchanges curriculum development would also include agreeing timetables and support needs such as childcare or other facilities (Ward and Taylor 1986, McGivney 1990). So the balance of power shifted to ensure that the learner's social context was neither assumed nor ignored. In these circumstances the learners, too, had authority to know.

The values on which higher education hangs its quality system (such as consistency of level, credit and assessment), simply did not apply on the community courses. Inevitably then, notions of progression didn't either (McGivney 1993). Progression, like the curriculum was evaluated for its lateral, rather than linear qualities. HOD1 was the only department head to describe progression in this way:

> This department are very keen on this what you might call more collective or social advance rather than an individual advance so something that the collective educational experience which actually enhances the life of the community in various tangible ways ... the group provides a kind of corporate or collective strength ... [which] don't have any necessary spin-offs in terms of ... individual advancement but do have a benefit for the whole community.

Although individual learners also identified personal gains on community courses it was often in relation to self esteem rather than linear credentials, as chapter nine shows.

The rejection of the 'bland and neutral' liberal approach for working class education has long since been critiqued (Jackson 1980, for example). The educational process of using experience as an analytical knowledge base, rather than a way of learning has also been claimed as a feminist position (Skeggs 1997, Henwood and Pidgeon 1995). Edwards (1999) does warn against lapsing into allowing universities to colonise experiential learning as a new 'regime of truth'. She suggests the concept of flexibility within experiential and lifelong learning discourses can lull learners into a false sense of empowerment. There is a danger of simply producing a heavily vocationalist skills curriculum: 'in the service of advanced capitalist economy' (p.268). Experiential knowledge is defended here, however, with echoes of Freire (1972), as a resource for analysing wider issues by drawing on the marginalised perspective. The ensuing discussion enhances and elaborates people's understanding of their social situation, and, thereby, the potential to change that situation (Taylor 1997). CA5, for instance, described a housing issues course for inner city tenants:

> You are looking at housing legislation, you're looking at housing finance, you are looking at housing organisation but you don't set up particular [curriculum] blocks and deal with this in a kind of mechanistic way that a lot of more formalised courses do. We are dealing with those same issues, contextualising, putting into a public policy context, putting it into a political context, but all the time relating it to their experience.

CA4 explained how he would teach such a session:

> I called it a tale of two multi-storey flats, because I had a flip chart of the flats they lived in in 1979 because some were, as you expect, actually coming out with: 'Problems in this area are down to bad tenants' and I said: 'Well look at these flats in 1979'; so we looked at the social conditions in 1979, you know, low unemployment, higher benefits, not that much higher, so we and then we compared them with now, you know, to show all the changes, rise in unemployment. So that was drawing on the experiences but relating it to the area.

There are two aspects of interest here. Firstly the content comes before the theory. The content is an extra-disciplinary issue rather than a single, or even multi-disciplinary, subject such as history or education or politics. Critique of the main issue draws on known concerns to the participants rather than subject matter from outside their experience. The second aspect is how that localised knowledge is used to create theory in the wider context of society, the social conditions in the 1990s. As Usher, Bryant and Johnston (1997) state: 'Student experience and 'voice' should not be taken at face value but educational efforts made to problematise, locate and evaluate them' (p.43). This way of examining knowledge, it is argued, enables marginalised groups to critically analyse because the questions are already relevant and give credence to their 'subjugated' or academically unrecognised knowledge. Many of the examples mentioned by the community academics were focused around the social circumstances of specific cultural groups. So CA3 explained how mothers would automatically use critical thinking skills in a mother and toddler group as they compared children's behaviour; I cited how Asian women would compare and critique teaching styles in Pakistan and England using knowledge which only they could provide. These examples highlight how the experiential knowledge of marginalised groups is easily ignored because

50

it is meaningless to the dominant way of seeing things (discourses). As a result text-based, and arguably, incomplete knowledge is legitimated without reference to the people most able to enhance it. One case in point was a course for disabled day centre users who were learning personal advocacy skills. They were invited to watch and comment on a cartoon video of the day in the life of a wheelchair users' attempt to obtain an adaptation for her bathroom.

> They were shown this video and they just reeled off a whole range of attitudinal issues as well as practical issues like ramps and things. They understood exactly what that video was about because it was about their lives. And the disabled tutor said it was really interesting; she said when she shows this video to able bodied professionals, all they notice is the lack of ramps and the lack of doors and things; they never notice the attitudinal things ... so it's something about doing it on their terms and giving the same status to that kind of experience and different kind of vocabulary (CA6).

This instance shows how certain groups can use their privileged view of the world (standpoint) to critique situations. As a result they enhance the knowledge base of those with authority to know - in this case by exposing the otherwise unnoticed behaviours associated with oppression.

It might be argued that such a curriculum is all well and good but should only be a first stage entry to more text based knowledge. The point to be made here, however, is not the course's lack of text content; rather that text, which is compiled by able bodied individuals, fails to include an awareness of the disability perspective (Oliver 1990). Bourdieu explained this in terms of cultural capital:

> The struggles between the symbolic system to impose a view of the social world defines the social space within which people construct their lives (in Harker et al 1990: 5).

The question of 'level' of analysis in such contexts as these simply does not apply. This level of analysis is only available outside the able-bodied world of text and scholarship. In the academic scheme of things, it is not even a rung on the ladder, despite the depth of awareness displayed amongst the participants compared to their educated professionals.

The experience curriculum and its relationship to critical analysis was a crucial element in the creation of courses. The mainstream academic (dominant) discourse disregards such insights because it simply does not notice them. Marginalised people's voices are selected out along with their insights, identities and different ways of knowing. The curriculum world of disciplinarity and learning addresses an abstracted and selective culture (Bird 1996, Lynch and O'Riordan 1998), through texts which talk to the tutor and not the students.

The remainder of this book attempts to give public space to those different learners. Each chapter takes on a particular strand of their being. Their individual life histories unfold to reveal complex lives. Caught between the expectations of their culture, class and generation, many undertook independent learning initiatives. Their invisibility from the mainstream was often a reflection of lives which were selected out of existence by people with authority to know. Others simply conformed to what was expected of them and were silenced out that way. But let the chapters explain and tell their own stories.

5 Setting the local scene - the learner contexts

> Social exclusion is ... multiple deprivation resulting from a lack of personal, social, political or financial opportunities ... Social inclusion [is] the attempt to integrate or increase the participation of marginalised groups within mainstream society (Barry 1998: 1).

Up to now we have looked at institutional power. I have claimed that the effect of institutional power is to marginalise difference in higher education, especially in relation to teaching and learning. I have argued that integration for the socially excluded must take account of their differentiated locality, social context and values. The focus in the ensuing chapters will now change to talking about the learners. This chapter places those learners in their wider social environments. Thirty people, with social backgrounds and views which are seldom heard in university continuing education, gave their life stories. Those stories are briefly sketched here as an introduction to the analysis which follows. The learners are divided into sub-groups to highlight shared cultural or social situations. The boundaries between the groups were not hard and fast. People shared common experiences across groups and had distinctively different backgrounds within the classification that I gave them. Nevertheless there were four cohorts of people who attended similar courses in their respective community settings and studied topics which were relevant to their specific social circumstances. The names and places of people are fictitious throughout to respect requests for anonymity. Their ages and circumstances relate to the time they were taking the courses between 1993 and 1995. The extent of their deprivation from educational opportunities would vary, as would the level of their participation in 'mainstream society'. The first group of learners all came from a small industrial town, which I have called Portside.

Portside

The people of Portside would probably not regard themselves as socially excluded, so much as geographically isolated. The town's economic fortunes and the experiences of certain individuals reflect, however, the state of flux which characterises the economic instability of some working class communities. Portside is a small town with a population of some 61,000. It grew substantially between 1870 and the early 1900s, primarily with mine and steel industries. There is one road into Portside. The next town is eight miles away and the nearest motorway link town is twenty miles away. As a remote location with a pre-1870 population of only a few hundred it experienced mass in-migration to service these industries. Portside residents today therefore have a shared history of migration and settlement. Most Portside inhabitants have married and stayed in the town for several generations. It is a relatively close-knit community whose male population, until recent mass redundancies, would expect to be employed in 'the yard' (P____) or associated industries. The majority of educational activities would therefore be craft or engineering oriented and male-centred. Although the County adult education service supports other local initiatives via schools and voluntary organisations, in 1991 neither the WEA nor university adult education had an established reputation in Portside. In terms of localised social capital, however, the town boasts a variety of societies, ranging from disability self help groups to a local history society.

Throughout its short history the town often experienced full employment, followed by troughs of unemployment, influenced by wider political or social factors. In 1988 unemployment was 10.5%. In 1994 it was 21.4%, reflecting the recent rapid decline of its main industrial base. It has a lower than average proportion of professional and intermediate (socio economic groups one and two) workers living in the town, with above average proportions of skilled, non-manual and skilled manual workers. Some 53% of the workforce are employed in the manufacturing sector and 40% engaged in the service sector.

During 1991/2 I made contact with individual professionals in the town, resulting in the occasional, termly employment one day a week of Karen as a local coordinator. Her goal was to develop courses which would be of university ethos but attract local interest amongst people who would not normally consider university education. Karen herself was born and bred in the town and knew the locality well. She worked in P____ till marriage and her husband worked at P____. News of mass redundancies had just been announced and the town was poised for a period of enforced leisure. Karen initiated a programme of short courses for adults, six per year, organising

54

venues, publicity, tutors and enrolment. Her first choice was a series of 14 hour family history courses run by her uncle Charles - a fellow Portsidean who had also started life in P____ as an apprentice. By 1992 he was a retired FE lecturer with his own consultancy business and taking an Open University science degree.

The family history courses attracted well over a hundred people. They were followed by a series of local history talks and then a more academic course by a tutor recommended to me from my University, called Monks, Mines and Men. After these courses I assisted with initial publicity to set up Portside's first ever Family History Society, organised by Charles and Karen and now with a membership of over two hundred people. Following on from these courses, Karen organised a series of lectures on antiques, astronomy talks, a politics course and, more recently some science courses for Age Concern. The course venues varied from a local church hall, a room in the library or the town's youth centre to a room in Age Concern. Karen's comments, recorded during 1993 are included in later chapters where it seemed relevant to do so. The community learners' backgrounds are summarised as follows:-

Gladys was the eldest woman in the study at 68 years old. She was the fifth of seven children and her story was contextualised by acute poverty and family ill health. Her father had a debilitating accident as a manual worker, leaving him unable to earn a steady income for his chronically ill wife. Gladys left school at the minimum leaving age, also in ill health, first to help her mother at home and later to earn some cash at a local factory. Within eighteen months, however, she had obtained a job at Marks and Spencers (commonly regarded as a 'good' job for girls) till her marriage, when she ceased work to bring up four children. It was not until she was in her forties, at the family doctor's suggestion, that she ventured back into paid work, this time as a demonstrator at an electrical firm. From there she was promoted, ending up in the office, managing stock flow and finances. Although she performed well at school she forfeited the opportunity to go to grammar school because of family circumstances. Her elder sister had already passed but been unable to go. In spite of a harsh childhood environment, Gladys talked affectionately of her parents, school and home, maintaining she had a happy and fulfilling life. All of Gladys' children stayed on at school, with the youngest entering higher education. Gladys had not pursued any formal education before the outreach programme, though she received work-related training.

Chris is Gladys' husband and at 70 was the oldest person in the study. He attended a Catholic school from five till the age of 14. He described a regular childhood routine of bringing his father's Sunday dinner into work during the double shift changeover period. He left school to work as an office boy in the shipbuilding industry until he was old enough to follow his father's footsteps into the ironworks, where he worked his way up during the war years and beyond, from fourth to second hand. He volunteered in his thirties as one of only two people to train for a new system of electric furnace work, returning to introduce the process in his home town and eventually, at the age of 42, changing his career to foreman in the local shipbuilding industry. Although he had received work-related training for the electric steel-making process and attended foreman's courses in his fifties, Chris never attended any other formal courses. Chris indicated a wide range of study interests from politics to the weather. He saw a notice about the family history course in his local church and decided that he and Gladys should go together.

Julie, now in her mid forties, had elected not to study commercial subjects at her secondary modern school, choosing to leave at age 15. Her career choice was shop work. She took a year's break at age 20, when she had her first child, returning to work part time at Marks and Spencers, where she has been for 24 years. She was happy with her career and did not feel educationally disadvantaged. Apart from work-related training she did not study as an adult till the family history course, though she regularly visited the library for leaflets and at the time of the study was considering doing some local history courses if the timing suited her other commitments. Julie talked less about her parents or immediate family than most of the participants but she did say she encouraged her own child and step son to get qualifications and pursue their education beyond school.

Margaret, the youngest of two, the daughter of a miner and wife of a tradesman has three daughters of her own. At 56 she was still of employable age but had not been in paid work since getting married, claiming that this was the norm till the 1960s. Margaret was the only person from Portside to have received a grammar education. She was, however, discouraged by her father from staying on beyond O level. She initially worked in her father's shoe shop but was then persuaded by him to work in his credit trading business. By the time she was sixteen, Margaret's mother had fallen ill, dying two years later. Margaret originally wanted to be a nurse but her father talked her out of it. She did not particularly want either of her school leaving jobs. Although she stressed she has enjoyed her life bringing up her three daughters, Margaret was more wistful than most about the loss of 'better opportunities' and a 'proper career'. As a result she ensured her own daughters stayed on at school; all three entered higher education. Some years ago she attempted one college pottery course and a 'free' psychology course which went with it. Margaret also used to enjoy attending trade union conferences with her husband when he was union representative. She had started reading independently about family history courses before seeing the community advert in the local press. Again, like Gladys, she attended with her husband and continued to attend subsequent local history courses.

Eric, at the age of 63 represents the largest age group of those who attended the Portside courses. He recalled not wanting to attend the grammar school in spite of being entered for the exam. However, Eric's memories of secondary modern school were unhappy and overshadowed by the violence of his teachers. Although his father wanted him to stay on beyond the age of 14, the local postmistress persuaded his father to let Eric enter the post office as a clerical worker. His father encouraged him to take post office exams by correspondence course till he was 18. Apart from two years national service Eric remained in the same occupation till early retirement. He had never attended any adult education courses before the community courses. He felt the opportunity to first discuss the course with Karen, the link worker, was a great motivating influence. Apart from bowls and an untapped interest in philosophy, Eric did not refer to any learning desires, though he mentioned accumulating books on all subjects. However, like the majority of participants, Eric had already started researching family history by borrowing library books on the subject. Despite a dislike of history at school his enthusiasm for the subject was now growing. He cited an interest in quizzes as one source of his awakened desire for knowledge. On the whole Eric was happy with his education, though he felt the school affected his self confidence and ability to speak in public.

Emma, aged 53, married with two children, was the only secondary modern pupil in the study to have stayed at school till she was sixteen. This enabled her to take commercial subject exams and obtain an office job immediately on leaving school, attending night school to gain further shorthand and typing qualifications. She felt her education had been good and she had worked to the best of her ability, once promoted to the A stream. Emma's daughter also took commercial subjects at school. In her twenties, Emma was offered promotion in a city approximately 120 miles away, but decided not to take it as she had recently become engaged. During her children's school years Emma worked in a shop and in school dinners, returning to office work at the age of 40. She had recently retired. The family history course was Emma's first venture into formal education since her early night school years. She was not particularly interested in attending anything else at that time. She once considered an Open University course, but dismissed the idea feeling she was not clever enough.

57

Emma did cite two relatives who were teachers, but described her own parents as 'not anything special' and 'not very clever'. She was happy with her choice of job and married life.

Muriel was the second oldest female in this study at 62. She was married with two children. She left school at 14. Although she felt her parents encouraged her education they did not allow her to take the grammar school exam. Muriel regretted this lost opportunity, but said she was happy with her ultimate career choices on leaving school, first as a confectioner apprentice - changing later, due to a flour allergy, to the jewellery trade. As an A stream pupil, Muriel had the opportunity of taking commercial subjects but declined. Apart from one flower arranging course and work-related management training, Muriel had not attended anything till the community courses, which - like Gladys and Margaret, she did with her husband. Muriel is now treasurer and membership secretary of the Family History Society, formed as a result of the course. One of her children entered higher education.

Graham, at the age of 31, was unrepresentative of the majority of participants in the community courses in Portside. Although he attended a technical school whose status was above secondary modern level, he only left school with two O levels and two CSEs. Graham completed a bricklaying apprenticeship with the town council and was still working for them in 1993. Like Chris he talked appreciatively of his trade. However, he was less complimentary about the support he received as a manual worker, compared with his office peers. In spite of being glad to leave school as soon as possible, Graham indicated an interest in libraries and described at length the stimulation he received from his continued family history research. He attended the course with his mother, though his wife now helps him and is equally enthusiastic about the subject. They had one child. The front room of their house served as an office and research base for their family history studies.

Peggy, aged 54 also attended the family and local history courses with her husband. The youngest of four from a mining family, her mother died when she was young and her father died when she was 19. She had eight children of her own, of whom three went to university. Her husband was public school educated and had recently retired as a teacher. Peggy's own career started with a series of factory jobs, although by 1993 she had been a medical clerk for seventeen years. Although she passed to go to the grammar school at the age of thirteen there were no places available. She still regretted this lost opportunity, although she spoke highly of her secondary education. Immediately on leaving school Peggy achieved two O levels by correspondence course while working shifts in a local factory.

She later took up Gaelic in her thirties. Whilst never having attended any formal adult education courses before the outreach programme, Peggy revealed a string of leisure pursuits from knitting to aerobics. She had already started her own family history search before the course and since attending the community courses did venture on her own into a publicised local history lecture at the library. Peggy described herself as being more keen than her peers to learn, with an interest in a variety of subjects. She was conscious of the difference in education between herself and her public-school educated, teacher husband. She saw the difference as a mark of inferiority, though she admitted to being good at her present job.

Sheila, at 40 was the youngest female from Portside to take part in this study. She was the only person to claim a B stream education throughout her secondary schooling. B stream pupils were not expected to study for exams even though they were now available in secondary modern schools. Surprisingly her father was a primary school deputy head and her mother a shorthand typist, giving her a much more middle class upbringing than the other course participants. Sheila was unhappy with the teaching quality of her school and the way it segregated her educational chances and subsequent career options. She would like to have been a beautician or 'something with cookery' but, with the limited options open to her, chose shopwork, received work-related training and progressed to head of department at Boots till her marriage. She chose not to return to work - though she had been helping at a local playgroup for ten years. Sheila had recently attended a computer course, which she eventually gave up through frustration at how the course was catering for men with some knowledge of computers rather than fulfilling its advertised commitment to beginners. In spite of some bad learning experiences, Sheila fluently articulated a belief in her potential ability to learn, given the appropriate learning environment and teaching approach.

The stories of the people from Portside indicated that social exclusion is not only heterogeneous but might be seen on several continua - of attitudes, circumstances and expectations. Some experienced more material disadvantage than others, but all cited at least one instance of exclusionary behaviour which influenced their personal attitude to education and their ambitions for their children.

The ability of the Portside residents to bridge the learning worlds which were available to them, contrasted relatively favourably with the efforts of the next group. These individuals lived in a different town and were all more or less associated with a day centre for people with disabilities. The day centre was called Wyrevale.

Wyrevale day centre

Wyrevale day centre is run by Social Services, catering for up to 60 people a day. At this time the centre consisted of two large rooms, one of which doubled up as a dining area, games and TV room with, when courses were offered, screened off class room space. The second room offered a range of craft activities. In addition to the day centre manager and her administrator, were a number of part time care staff who helped with meals, transport and general care needs. The day centre has a regular routine. People with a variety of disabilities and ages attend at the same time each week. They are transported to and from their homes by social services transport. Sometimes trips out are organised. At other times special events are brought in, of which the community courses represented one aspect. The centre has been operating for several years and draws its catchment from a ten mile radius.

Unemployment for the locality during the 1990s was above the regional average at 8.9%. Hosting two higher education institutions, and with a population of just over 123,000, the area provides evidence of both affluence and subsistence level activity. On the other hand a working class culture draws its heritage largely from former textile industries and farming. Some of this heritage has been replaced by more acute forms of socio economic deprivation. Homelessness and drug addiction are on the increase, though mostly situated in the nearby seaside town - where unemployment rates fluctuate and where people often congregate in the hope of work during the summer. Bed sits and boarding accommodation are common in that town. It consequently suffers from a non-static population with only seasonal employment. Tourism is usually confined to low pay day trippers. Its neighbouring university town fares better, able to promote sites of historic interest and attract passing trade from people making a detour from the motorway. It is also a popular town for middle class retired professionals. The ethnic minority population is small, at just over 1,000 people.

During 1991 and 1992 I made contact with Wyrevale through a network organisation run by social services (the SST) and chaired by Lesley a local minister who also used a wheelchair. In view of its proximity to my work base I remained the centre's main contact for course development until 1995. I discussed with the SST contacts and Wyrevale's day centre manager, Rachel, the range of options which might be possible under the programme's remit. It was agreed that in addition to providing discipline-specific, general interest courses I would work with the SST and interested service users in developing and teaching courses which addressed committee work skills, local authority liaison and community development skills. I devised and taught a committee skills course and personal development course, with tailor made syllabi around these remits. Although they were ostensibly open courses they were specifically advertised to Wyrevale members and other disabled contacts through the SST. The ultimate aim was for the participants to take a lead role in creating a user forum, which Mavis, a disabled professional trainer, was responsible for initiating via Social Services. In the event, Mavis obtained a new job shortly after the course completion and the user forum gradually folded.

Most courses were offered in the day centre and its users' second home, now called SCOPE. The courses at SCOPE were advertised locally and did attract a small number of local residents as well as SCOPE members. Early in 1994 one short transactional analysis course was also offered to Wyrevale people to take place at the university, with transport laid on. Subsequent to this stage funding restrictions created a break in continuity, though some courses still run in Wyrevale.

The Wyrevale group had a variable stock of life history experiences on which to draw in their adult lives. Oppenheim (1998) describes positive past experiences as necessary assets if people are to overcome marginalisation: 'Assets represent past investment and the individual/family/community's ability to weather the storms of, say unemployment, separation, illness or disability' (p.21). Every Wyrevale member experienced all these storms, though the level of their past investments influenced the here and now to differing degrees.

Phyllis was married at 17 divorced, remarried and now separated from her second husband. She was the eldest of four and her parents worked in a restaurant as a child. Aged 46 now she had one son and longstanding ambitions to go to art college. She described an unhappy and abusive childhood with her own parents getting divorced when she was 15. Although she started a hairdressing apprenticeship on leaving school, she gave this up to work in a factory and support her mother financially after the separation. More recently she had been a home help. After a cancer operation seven years ago she had been attending Wyrevale for four years. In spite of little parental support from her parents, she said her father thought education was very important. Phyllis stated she was keen to attend courses but generally did not complete those she did attend at the local college - such as pottery and a counselling course. She attended Wyrevale's committee skills course and was a member of Wyrevale's users committee.

Mandy acquired a road accident injury to her leg as a child. This turned into arthritis in the early 1980s and she had been attending Wyrevale for about eight years. Mandy was brought up a Catholic in Belfast, though at the age of 45 was still able to remember Northern Ireland before the troubles. She described the pre-troubles oppression of poverty that Catholics suffered in Northern Ireland, manifested in the limited availability of jobs as well as housing, shops and school facilities. Like the others Mandy left school without qualifications and, the eldest of a large family, took up a local factory job at the age of 15. She left Ireland in 1967 with her army husband. After his medical discharge they settled in Lancaster where her two sons went to the local grammar school and one entered university. She spent most of her married life doing cleaning jobs to help make ends meet while her husband worked in an office. Both she and her husband were ambitious that their children would have a better education than they did, but Mandy was less interested for herself, claiming that her state of health would make regular learning impossible.

Joan was the second eldest of the Wyrevale group at the age of 57. She was educated in a small farming village. One of eleven children she left at 15 to do farmwork and bring money into the family. At the age of 20 a rare disease gradually impaired her mobility and sight. She left farming to work in a cotton factory, her parents dying meanwhile during her late twenties. She married at 36 years and has two children. She had been attending Wyrevale for the last fifteen years and was recently widowed. Joan revealed an exceptionally shy personality, which her school tried hard to help her overcome by giving her small responsibilities such as looking after the milk round in order to bring her out of herself. Whilst Joan attended and enjoyed a confidence building course, she expressed little enthusiasm for more courses, preferring to play dominoes. Nevertheless the experience encouraged her to become involved in the local church and its social events. One of her children attended grammar school and both went on to further education.

Paul at 37 was the youngest of this group of participants and the only non-Wyrevale member. He was married but with no children. Like Gillian and Carol he has cerebral palsy and like Gillian spent several years of his childhood in and out of hospital. He had only been in a wheelchair for the last few years. Paul's primary school education started off in a state school, where he was badly bullied for being disabled. After two years of hospital operations he was taught at home from the age of nine to eleven. Thereafter he went to a state boarding school for pupils with special needs till he left at sixteen. Although he felt generally better cared for at the special school he did not enjoy being isolated 'miles from anywhere' and was aware that the curriculum limited his education. Paul had done a series of labouring jobs since leaving school. He fought and won two separate unfair dismissal claims during his working life and continued to find his own employment till the age of 28. When jobs became more difficult to find his doctor then signed him on for invalidity benefit and he has not worked since. Paul was chairman of a regional Disabled Drivers Association and member of a local Access Federation. He felt the personal skills course increased his confidence to tackle authority figures. Paul did try one or two college courses but was put off by access difficulties and a general lack of confidence in his own ability to sit for a long time or attend regularly.

Tony was 55 years old and had been unemployed for six years at the start of his involvement in the community courses. He was brought up by his grandparents. Tony spoke fondly of them, saying they taught him discipline and to care for others. He himself had been married twice but now lived alone. Tony had no good memories of school saying the teachers had their pets for extra curricular activities and weren't interested in the rest. He enjoys practical subjects and went into textile and building trades on leaving school. Tony's work history from the age of 16 to 43 was interspersed with accidents and various industrial job changes every few years. His leg amputation, replaced by a prosthetic eight years ago, prevents him from climbing stairs and he felt unable to adapt himself to a more sedentary job. Tony insisted that he was entirely self taught. He half completed a college course but was unhappy with the tutor. He admitted to being lonely and valuing course attendance partly for the opportunity to meet people. He attended the committee skills, confidence building and personal skills courses. Tony felt valued at Wyrevale where he called bingo numbers and where he could help other people. He spent his time offering printing services to people as a hobby and was slowly researching prosthetics and their origins.

Susan was 54. She left school at fifteen and acquired Crones disease at the age of 30. She was otherwise free from disability until her stroke at the age of 43. Susan described herself as shy and unconfident since childhood. She and her brother were bullied by their peers. Like her mother, Susan did cleaning while her children were young, though she originally worked in a clothing factory till her marriage at 21. Later she also did waitress work. She proudly described her father's well known skills as a pipe layer. She told of how his stubborn streak once brought him into conflict with his employer, resulting in him walking out of that job, only to get another job the following day with a rival firm. Susan emphasised how girls weren't encouraged to consider education or a career, both by her parents and the school. She admitted to being frustrated but 'never said owt' because 'you didn't in them days'. Susan likes practical subjects and always wanted to be a hairdresser. Her daughter is a nurse and her son, whilst unresponsive at school is now doing well in the RAF. Susan had been going to Wyrevale for fourteen years. But only in the last year or so had she decided to become proactive towards her own life there. She attended the committee skills and the personal skills course. She was very pleased at her recent achievement after the course in reviving the centre's stroke club at Wyrevale, even chairing the first meeting.

Carol age 51, was one of four children and has cerebral palsy. She was unmarried and shared her deceased father's house with a sister. Her father was a gardener and her brother obtained a degree as a mature student. Although she attended one of the local grammar schools Carol left at sixteen without taking any exams on the advice of the head teacher and her doctor, because her arm was 'getting more shaky'. Carol would have liked to do nursing but felt this was out of the question in view of her condition. She worked in the same shop for eighteen years until the new management put so much pressure on her that she became ill and was dismissed. Although she received compensation for unfair dismissal, a string of unsuccessful attempts to get another job knocked her confidence so much she became ill again. She had been at Wyrevale for eighteen years. She admitted she was very different now from her younger, happy-go lucky days before her illness. Although she attended three community courses she was not particularly interested in attending more courses. She was very conscious of her disability and felt most able bodied people 'don't like to see people like us'.

Dave was 48. He was brought up by his father, uncle, three brothers and grandparents in a pit village. The son of a mining family his mother died in childbirth when he was two. Both his school and home background contained stories of bullying and violence, mainly from his father and fellow pupils. At thirteen he was sent to approved school for petty theft, where his formal education virtually stopped. Dave had a very low self image, derived from his school days and resulting in little attempt to do anything for himself as an adult. On leaving school at fifteen or sixteen (he couldn't remember) Dave spent a few months in a variety of jobs till he was eighteen. He was unable to take his first choices of mining or the army because of a hearing impairment. After a brief spell in prison for petty theft he worked as a labourer till his brain haemorrhage at the age of 29 when he was confined to a wheelchair for two years. He now has a slight walking impairment, hearing problems and suffers from epilepsy. Before arriving at Wyrevale eight years ago, Dave was serving some sort of supervision order which entailed living in 'trust house' accommodation round the country. He still wrote to his ex-wife and children, but lived on his own. He had been coming to Wyrevale since his release from the supervision order seven years earlier. After attending the community courses Dave started joining committees and other organisations run by disabled people. He remarked he would never have considered adult education if it had not been brought to him. He attended all four courses provided through the community programme.

Henry was the oldest man in this group at 56 and the most recently disabled from a stroke eleven months before the community courses started. His background was atypical of the other interviewees. He came from a close-knit Methodist, farming family and was educated at a private Quaker school from where some pupils went onto Oxbridge. Henry's mother and wife were both teachers and one of his daughters also intended to teach. Also unlike his Wyrevale peers, Henry had a wide circle of school, family and farming contacts and drew on recent work experience. In spite of this pedigree, Henry left school without qualifications. He joined his father's farm at 16, later running his own until two years earlier when he sold up to clear off mounting debts. He worked more recently as a gardener and then a security officer. He still hoped to return eventually to work. Henry explained he did not sit school exams because he and his triplet brother were of a nervous disposition and unable to cope with exam stress. As a farmer he would attend sales reps talks on new farming technology, held at the university and elsewhere. Although he had no knowledge of 'how to go about it' the idea of adult education appealed to him, especially if it would help his job prospects. Henry attended the confidence building course soon after his stroke and the longer, personal development course a few months later.

In many respects this was the most disparate of all the groups to interview. The participants' disability status meant they were often channelled through social services as a cohesive sector of society with little consideration of individual needs or backgrounds. Having said this there were distinctive, identifying, socio economic features about many (though not all) of the participants' lives, which is an apparent feature of day centre regulars (Barnes 1993).

Nine of the ten participants recorded here were regulars at Wyrevale. Two professionals (wheelchair users) had been sessional tutors on one course. Whilst Mavis was not local, Lesley was; she knew the centre well and some of the participants on an individual basis as part of her own church and disability support roles in the community. The nature of the centre's provision means that all users are unemployed and few have any expectations of re-employment, irrespective of their age. They are therefore socially excluded by all available criteria. Perhaps the most interesting aspect of these stories is the extent to which the Wyrevale group built their own social networks and shared values - through the centre and their other, disability related, activities. These activities, however, received little acknowledgement by way of 'social capital'. On the other hand, if, as Schuller and Burns (1999) suggest, social capital is also evidenced by the extent of parental investment in their children's education, some members of this group were particularly disadvantaged. These observations will be discussed later, particularly under the themes of 'identity' and 'subjugated knowledge'.

The final two groups of learners came from different parts of a county I am calling Loamshire and were all women of Asian origin. Their complexity in relation to understanding notions of social exclusion become apparent in terms of class, culture, family relationships, education, religion and ambitions.

Loamshire

The particular influence of the women's cultural and religious backgrounds necessitate a few words of explanation concerning the Muslim and Hindu religions and cultural practices in the countries from which they originated. Most of this information was taken from County Council fact sheets and is interspersed with the women's own stories.

There were differences in their homeland educational practices from those in England. Schooling from the age of 10 was single sex and post 16 school leaver qualifications had to be passed en bloc, as a 'matriculation' exam, like the English School Certificate system of the 1930s. Colleges in Pakistan and India would be single sex, and the assumed location for A levels plus first degree study. Universities were generally for postgraduate study only.

The participant experiences in these two groups indicated that school facilities varied considerably. Whilst some villages had school classes of only 15 or 20, this might mean the teacher would be teaching two classes at once, with few facilities such as desks. In other cases class sizes might number 50, again influencing the style and nature of lessons. Private schooling was available in the more affluent towns and two Indian women were taught through this system. Whatever the circumstances, however, education was always highly valued. There were also indications that educational advancement is progressing rapidly across the Indian Sub-continent.

The climate, too had its influence on dress, food and social behaviours. All these differences, as well as similarities with the Wyrevale and Portside groups will become apparent as the stories unfold and their experiences mesh with attitudes and traditions in their respective English towns.

Loamshire X and Loamshire Y are different towns, approximately thirty miles apart. Unemployment in these areas was running at around 10% though for minority ethnic communities this increased to 17% in some locations.

Loamshire X

Loamshire X is a small town with a population of approximately 10,000. Some 20% are Muslim, the first settlements arriving in the 1960s from North Pakistan. Muslims in Loamshire X come primarily from the Punjab in Pakistan or the Gujarat state in India. As with most Asian religions, Islam represents a social system and way of life as well as a religion. It operates across regions, with laws and traditions for most aspects of individual, family and community life. Many features of Western secular culture and lifestyles conflict with the Islamic lifestyle, such as integration of the sexes, use of alcohol, gambling and extra marital relations. Mosques are primarily a place of worship for men and do not therefore serve the same community contact point for women. Islamic law gives men and women equal, but different, roles and responsibilities in the home and few Muslim women go out to work, though the activities of the participants in this study suggest that tendency is changing. The central place of the family and its good name are paramount to most Asian groups. Marriages are generally seen as a union between two whole families, and organised as a social, rather than individual arrangement. Divorce, whilst permitted, is heavily discouraged for both Muslims and Hindus. Although less common than amongst Hindus, dowries are also a feature of many Asian Muslim marriages.

Loamshire X community centre has been used since the early 1980s by its local Further Education college to run English classes, supported by crèche facilities, for Asian women. Some of the women come via college provided transport, others walk to the centre. During 1991/2 I established contact with the college, the local voluntary service council and a range of Asian community groups in the area. After a number of taster sessions a planned programme of bilingually led health and welfare rights courses were taught alongside the college's English language (ESOL) classes and with shared use of its crèche facilities. The university paid for Punjabi speaking subject specialists (usually identified through college contacts), while the college paid for ESOL tutor support and publicity mechanisms. The welfare rights and health courses ultimately led to a College foundation

67

award and were attended by women who had received little or no education in England. In addition, a short assertiveness course was offered. Subsequent to this study, a range of bilingually taught Islamic studies topics have been provided through the university's own foundation credit system as progression opportunities for some women. Six women and Afsar, the welfare rights tutor from this group contributed to this study. Afsar took responsibility for talking to the welfare rights course participants and translating their contributions.

Sanam was 25 in 1993. She had one son and had been in England nearly six years. She left full time study at seventeen after unexpectedly failing some exams in her first year at college. She was the middle child of nine children and lived in a small town in Gujarat. Her town environment meant her parents were relatively middle class with civil servant family connections. Unlike all the other Loamshire women, Sanam did work in Gujarat for eighteen months as a primary school teacher, continuing with her studies part time. This ceased with her marriage and move to England to live with in-laws. Having experienced quite a lot of freedom in Gujarat, she expressed many regrets at this move and the consequent restrictions on her life in England. These were imposed largely by her in-laws who had limited education and more traditional values towards women than she was used to. Although she and her husband had recently chosen to live in a separate house, she did still believe in the principle of extended family living. Her husband supported her wishes to attend classes and increase her independence. She still had aspirations to return to work and taught Urdu and Arabic privately to children at home. Initially Sanam came to the community centre for English classes on invitation from one of the other participants, but she joined the welfare rights course 'to see how it goes'. The course had increased her confidence and she intended to continue studying. She had joined the library and reads Urdu and English books.

Hinaa at 20 was the youngest participant. She was actually born in England but her father sent the family to Pakistan when she was six in order to learn the Islamic way of life and to know the Pakistan culture. Hinaa had only been back a few months and stated that 'People in Pakistan are far freer than what they are in England'. She was able to attend a girls high school in her Punjab village, but though educated to O level further studies were halted because of internal family fighting within the village. She returned to England for one year at the age of eighteen, then went back to marry her husband, though she had not yet lived with him because he was in prison as a result of the village riots. Hinaa's father spent some time in Denmark and England during her childhood but was very keen on education, only bringing the family all back to this country because of the troubles. He was even prepared to pay privately for her continued studies. Hinaa said that contrary to tradition, women were now starting to study in Pakistan towns after their marriage, if they had money and before they had children. Although women rarely work in Pakistan, she felt there might be a possibility for her in England and wanted to be a nursery nurse. She accepted she would never get permission to go to university and therefore did not strive for it. Hinaa felt she could understand English very well but lacked confidence in speaking it. She tried to improve her English by watching TV. Other times were spent on housework, living with her family, looking after her younger brothers and sisters and reading their school books.

Sabia, like Sara, came from a rural village in Jhelum near the Punjab in Pakistan. Although it was not common for girls in her village to go to secondary school, she was allowed to attend one close by. She left at sixteen, having gained the equivalent to O levels, and was now 22. Sabia did not go to college in Pakistan as this was not a common feature in her village, although she would like to have gone. She married at nineteen, has been in England three years and did not yet have children. All her cousins were also in England. One sister remained in Pakistan with her farming family. Her husband had been well educated in England and was a college lecturer. Although two other women reported that their fathers left home to work abroad, Sabia stipulated that her parents separated, leaving her maternal grandmother to influence her education. Sabia now lived in England just with her husband who supported her interest in further study. Like all the Muslim women Sabia valued the Islamic principles she learnt as a child, but unlike some still believed that education should be taught in context and with caution: 'Education can lead you astray if you are exposed to different people and different environments'. Sabia, too, only discovered the welfare rights course by attending English classes. She had never worked but continued to improve her English by watching TV and reading her nephews' school books.

Sara was 25 and had been in England ten years. Although she lived in a village in Jhelum, secondary schooling for girls was the norm, as there was a school available within the village itself. Her father had a professional job and some of her relatives had been to university. With some private coaching from her father Sara took her O level equivalents a year early, leaving school at fifteen and marrying the following year in England. She had four children and lived in an extended family. Sara too, regretted leaving her education so early and still had aspirations to go to university. Although she supported the Islamic principles for life she disagreed that females would 'go astray' if they studied away from home. She felt there should be places for women in England where they can study without compromising Islamic values. In common with a number of the Muslim women, she also commented on how girls who were brought up here have a different way of thinking. Sara had never done paid work. She looked after her invalid mother-in-law as well as her children. Until the welfare rights course she had not been to classes as an adult. Now her children were at school and with the experience of this course behind her, she was keen to progress and felt she now had the support of her in-laws to do so. Again, like many of the Loamshire women she tried to improve her English at home by reading her children's books and watching television. She also continued to read Urdu books and was a member of the library.

Aliya, at 33 was one of the oldest Loamshire women in this study. Mainly due to her father's interest in education she stayed at her Muslim village school in Gujarat till the age of fourteen, having learnt very little English and married at fifteen. Her husband was partially educated in England and came over to Pakistan to marry. She had now been in England eighteen years. Aliya had her first child at seventeen and now had six children. Although she reflected wistfully on her pressure-free childhood back in the Gujarat village of Dingar, she was committed to the responsibilities of motherhood along with the Islamic way of life and its values. She lived with her in-laws, including her husband's brother's families, valuing the relationships of an extended family. Although she had not worked independently, Aliya occasionally helped in her husband's grocer shop and cooked home-baked food to sell. She specifically chose not to go out to work, feeling it was important as a mother to be at home for her children. She attended English classes off and on for several years, when crèche facilities were available and family commitments permitting. At one stage she gained an O level in Urdu from the local college. Her goal in learning English was so she could support her children's schooling and 'get by' with everyday needs without an interpreter. Like the other women she read her children's books as a means of learning English at home. In spite of feeling happy with her life she did regret leaving school at such an early age to get married. Her main issue was the sense of dependency she still felt on other people due to language difficulties, though she acknowledged things were much easier than they were eighteen years ago.

Ruksana's educational background was the least common amongst the participants in this study. In her agricultural village children were educated till the age of nine. Whilst some boys might go out of the village to study further, girls remained at home and learned the Koran, housework and sewing. At a later stage a girls school was built in Ruksana's village and

70

her father paid for a year's private tuition from one of the school teachers for herself and her sister. Ruksana's father had in fact come to England when she was very young and the family followed when she was nearly fourteen. Ruksana did attend a special school in England for eighteen months to learn some basic English words. She returned to Pakistan in 1986 to marry at the age of sixteen. She came back to England a year later without her husband. It took five more years to obtain his visa, during which time she visited him once. Ruksana's husband is the only one from the Loamshire participants to have been entirely educated in Pakistan. As a result she was the main interpreter in her family. She was now 24, had been in England seven years and lived with her two children and husband. Ruksana supported the Pakistan way of life and her education, pointing out that in a village such as hers education was a luxury which was encouraged but which came second to daily economic survival and everyone in the village supporting each other. Both Ruksana and her husband were keen for their children to receive an education. Her husband supported Ruksana's efforts to study, recognising his own poor literacy, partly as a result of persistent truancy in Pakistan. Ruksana received no English lessons in Pakistan so she was largely self-taught. Like the others she also learned from television and her children's books.

Loamshire Y

The Hindu population in Loamshire Y originates from East Africa or Gujarat which lies between India and Pakistan. The participants came from rural villages, or small towns in the Gujarat state. As with Islam, Hinduism influences social relationships and general behaviour more consistently than Christianity now does in the West (though, of course, many English laws and patterns of behaviour originated from Christian principles). The practice of Hindu religions has many regional variations but is based on a philosophical acceptance of reincarnation where your present caste or status relates to actions in a previous existence. Future release from your station in life depends on how virtuously you live in the present. Life of any kind should not be destroyed. Hindu worship takes place mainly in the home, though there are now several temples (Mandirs) for congregational worship. In English towns these temples are an important source of community cohesion. Whilst the caste system is no longer strictly adhered to in its original status, it still influences social interaction, choice of marriage partners and even which temple to attend for worship. The caste system in Britain operates broadly according to this country's social class hierarchies and relates to wealth, education and occupation. As is the case for Muslims,

71

the extended family is an important feature of new marriages and the common pattern is for the wife to live at least initially with her husband's family and parents. In Hindu society, marriage is accompanied by a dowry from the daughter's parents to the in-laws. Again, as for most East Asian groups, there is a stronger tendency towards separation of the sexes for most social activities than in Western society.

Loamshire Y is a much larger town with its own university and hosting most of the UK's major shops. With a population of 126,000 its ethnicity is relatively diverse; Asian or black groups make up 10.3% of the population, of which 78% are of Indian Sub Continent origin. There is a Hindu population of approximately 5,000 and there are a number of Hindu temples in the town.

Courses in Loamshire Y started in 1993, initiated by the town's main Hindu community centre (HCC). The workers had seen an article by me in the local voluntary service newsletter inviting people to take part in my programme. The HCC is located in a converted school, comprising its temple, an administrative base, youth and community facilities and a women's education and training project. It forms the cornerstone for publicity, guidance and recruitment for a range of women's leisure and training courses. Between 1993 and 1994 I arranged two fifty hour courses. They were broadly described as personal development courses and consisted of assertiveness training, communication and job preparation skills. Again the courses were for women who had not been educated in England and were taught bilingually. The HCC undertook all recruitment and publicity arrangements and identified their own Gujarati speaking tutors, though I tracked down the bilingual assertiveness tutor via an assertiveness training organisation. Four women and two tutors, Amita and Kajal, contributed to this study. Kajal translated for the HCC course participants.

Madhun was the only course participant to have a degree, completed in India, along with some typing courses before getting married at the age of 23. Madhun had five brothers and sisters, all of whom were well educated. Before leaving India she did clerical work for a short while in her father's business. She was now 25 and had been in England for two years. Madhun stated that her in-laws, with whom she still lived, as well as her husband were encouraging her to pursue courses in England. They supported her desire for a career and interest in a range of academic and practical studies, including learning to drive and swim. Her husband's family, including the women, have professional jobs and Madhun still hoped for a professional career in England. She had done a number of computer and work experience courses and her English was more advanced than most. Madhun wanted to be stretched. She appreciated the community personal development course because it challenged her thinking. She was the only person to hint that failed attempts to obtain a job in England might relate to her race, rather than ability.

Vijayanti was 25 years old. The daughter of a Hindu police superintendent and the only girl in a family of four, she studied commerce at high school and college in India but married before completing her A levels. She had studied English for three years but on arrival in England spent most of her working life in factory or unskilled jobs with no opportunity to develop her knowledge of English. She had been in England for about six years and had three children. Only since she recently gave up work, due to ill health, had she begun attending courses, ranging from henna painting to computer training. Vijayanti lived with her in-laws and struggled to obtain support from both her husband and in-laws for her studies. She was very keen to improve herself, grateful for the opportunities in this country and felt that even if further education did not lead to a job for herself, at least she could use it to help improve her children's future. During any spare time she tried to revise her course notes and read English magazines. Vijayanti emphasised the importance of the local temple and community centre as an information resource for Asian women to find out about courses - and the importance of her tutor, who lived in the same community, to act as a role model for her. She felt the assertiveness training aspect of the community course had built up her confidence and she subsequently encouraged other women to attend classes.

Shivani, one of the youngest at 20 was a friend of Vijayanti's. She had been in England eighteen months. She was one of only two children. Her brother attended a private school and both her parents-in-laws had professional jobs. Shivani only completed one year of her A level studies in England before getting married and coming to England. She still lived with her in-laws but gained most support from her husband, who was educated in England and had a good job here. He helped her learn English and had even told her to train for the next three or four years till they decided to have children. Shivani had career aspirations though she felt guilty about not bringing in any money while she studied. She had done computer courses at college as well as the community centre. She practised her English at home by listening to tapes, reading and practising her spelling. Again she kept others informed about classes being run through the temple/community centre. Like the others she appreciated the assertiveness course because it helped her to stand up for herself.

Shila was also 25 and had two brothers, one of whom was qualified to degree level. She had been in England for six years. She came from a professional family background and attended a private school in India, intending to study to degree level. Like Vijayanti she too studied as far as the first year at college, leaving at 18 to get married just after taking her A level equivalents. Although she asked her England-educated husband if she could stay in India to complete her studies he chose to return to this country. She had two children and had recently moved away from living with her in-laws. Shila's husband worked in a travel shop and was encouraging her to attend courses at the community centre. Shila's employment pattern was similar to Vijayanti's. She currently had a part-time cleaning job but was still keen to pursue a teaching career. Shila expressed regret about her lost opportunity in India, though she admitted to being ready to get married. The community course was her first experience of education in this country and she was very keen to continue with further courses. She, too, went over study notes at home and she too felt a responsibility to encourage other female members of the local Hindu community to take up opportunities offered to them.

Religious influences notwithstanding, perhaps the most significant features of difference from the West for these women are the geographical distinctions in size, climate and infrastructure in the country of origin. All these have strong social and economic implications for personal expectations and impinge on people's belief systems in the West. India and Pakistan cover a vast area of diverse regions. Geographical location determines the availability and range of schooling and work opportunities more sharply than in the UK (though again there were trends in the Portside and Wyrevale interviews which indicated similar links between educational attitude and economic progress). It was not uncommon for people to receive private, and costly, tuition when more formal systems were not in place. Some small isolated villages consisted of landowners whose economic survival depended on unmechanised agriculture in an uncertain climate. Attitudes in these locations were often conservative and traditional. Small towns, however, operate with different and changing social and regional traditions. Yet other towns have international infrastructures, with consequent attitudes towards education.

The community education goal for both groups was to enhance and complement existing provision, encourage the use of bilingual, role model tutors and view analytical content, rather than language as the key learning focus. Although the community education programme has since provided courses for women of Asian heritage who were educated in England, nearly all the participants in these courses were 'newly arrived'. Their responses reflect that perspective and should not be seen as representative of the majority of women born and brought up in this country, as the tutors and

74

participants themselves highlighted. Nevertheless, Pakistani and Indian heritage families maintain close ties with the homeland across generations and the tradition of bringing wives into this country for marriage continues, with resultant effects on each new generation born in this country. It is common, for instance, for family members to return to Pakistan or India for several months or even years.

Schuller (1998, 1998a) and Schuller and Burns (1999) identify some key features of social capital as demonstrating high levels of trust and mutuality, shared values and norms for collective purpose, rather than self interest, and a strong network of social relations, through which information and ideas flow. Whilst these traits were differentially evident amongst Portside and Wyrevale learners, the Loamshire group in particular indicated a strong sense of social cohesion across all facets. This should have meant a high parental investment in education and consequent high income in the labour market. Their (overseas) educational qualifications did place some of them beyond the educational achievements of the Portside and Wyrevale groups, but it is significant that their social capital did not materialise into social inclusion in this country. In other words, only certain forms of social networks and values have recognised worth in the dominant discourse for equity. The effects of gender, race, class and disability would play their part in defining social capital and strategies for social inclusion.

This chapter has outlined the social and organisational context for the university community education programmes and for each group of community participants. The various locations provide a backdrop to the stories supplied by the learners. The next two chapters dissect the above stories to show how individual lives were moulded to suit much wider agendas.

6 Excluded versions of truth

There remain aspects of social exclusion which are under-researched, such as participation in political and voluntary organisations, involvement in education (both formal qualifications or evening classes), access to financial services, the extent of networks of friendship and wider social networks, self perceptions, sense of self esteem or identity ... Perhaps most importantly we don't know much about the dynamics and inter-relationships between different forms of exclusion and the ways in which they may reinforce each other (Oppenheim 1998: 21).

Chapter four showed that community staff in universities had limited power to change the system from within in ways which would support their learners. There were also issues of power which operated outside the system and amongst the marginalised themselves. Closer analysis of the learners' stories highlights some of the dynamics and inter-relations which have shaped their educational decision making. The stories reveal that exclusion is a relative term; but the experience of exclusion is about power relationships and the capacity of agents of power (family, professions etc) to control other people's lives (Mulgan 1998).

Whilst later chapters show people could resist such domination, this and the next chapter build up a picture of the cumulative effects of power and agency, revealing that truth is multifaceted with many hidden realities. Dominant truths would often influence how people perceived and responded to their own social realities, particularly in relation to a sense of educational entitlement. Different age groups, for example, often demonstrated similar perceptions of non entitlement to higher education in the context of their particular economic, cultural or socially driven circumstances. So whilst people revealed different educational arguments over time in relation to their social circumstances the legacy of earlier expectations often lingered, producing new rationalities for maintaining old differentials.

Link workers or tutors would supplement the learners' stories. From their between-culture position they would explain the learner positions in ways which both challenged higher education and sometimes challenged the learners. As a result they demonstrated how viewpoints shift and how new attitudes come into play as discourses (behaviours, attitudes, belief systems) gradually intermingle.

This chapter looks at how discourses have historically influenced working class and other relationships with higher education. Between them the learners spanned three generations. Schooling for the Asian women ranged from private education to basic elementary schooling depending on family circumstances. Schooling for others included the war years and periods just before and after the 1944 Education Act in England. Their stories are introduced here collectively according to their participant locations.

Portside

With the exception of Sheila, whose father was a teacher, the parents of all the Portside members had skilled or semi skilled manual occupations. Whilst some women married men without manual occupations, all expressed in some way an affiliation with their 'working class town'. Within this framework most did relatively well in their careers. Karen, the link worker, and in her forties, was very much part of the social history of the people on whose behalf she negotiated the courses. The seven women learners, plus Karen, had all progressed in terms of work responsibilities from their first job in a factory or shop. Tutor Charles, too, followed initially the career path of many of his contemporary male students. They all, for instance, undertook some form of apprenticeship though Charles subsequently took an open university degree in early retirement. Only Margaret (age 56) who attended a grammar school, and Graham, the youngest in his thirties, left school with O levels or CSEs. All were married. All had children, and five participants cited children who had studied beyond A level. None had been to university themselves and only two of them knew that universities offered courses to adults. All were brought up in Portside and all, except Emma and Graham, attended further community courses after their initial family history course. None of the learners was attending courses elsewhere at the time of the university's involvement and some had not studied formally for over thirty years.

The majority of the participants' comments reflect current literature on working class images of school, family and work of the time (Roberts 1984, 1993, Bourke 1994). That is, family circumstances were often hard:

> There were a lot of people that had brains that weren't encouraged to use them, they just had to get out and earn money as quickly as possible. For one thing there were very big families and the oldest ones had to get out to work to help support the young ones (Muriel, age 62).

77

Although education was often valued, people were more concerned with finding a job and fulfilling a sense of collective responsibility for the family. Schools would respect that position and allow people to leave for that purpose (Roberts 1995, Jackson & Marsden 1973). Chris said, for instance:

> The year before I left school they'd just raised the school leaving age from fourteen to fifteen, and at that time anybody who could find a job that was over fourteen, between fourteen and fifteen, could apply for an exemption to leave school, and these were usually granted if the person had a job to go to (age 70).

Lynch and O'Riordan (1998) claim that even today the principal working class influences on educational decision making are economic, social, cultural and educational. It is not surprising then that each generation in this group cited an interrelationship between those factors on their own learning histories. So schools would collude in the cultivation of a social world which prepared boys for a certain role in 'the yard':

> I went to the technical school, so like as soon as you went in, because me dad says well that's you in P_____ anyway, because, you know, so like all through school life it was am I going to be a fitter, a turner, electrician or am I going to be a draughtsman? Really and that was sort of school life. It didn't really matter about your exams because you went to the technical school you were into P_____ (Graham, age 31).

Girls were prepared for motherhood. Sheila's comments specifically made this point: 'They educated you more to be a housewife and mother, you know cookery and sewing and things like that' (Sheila, age 40). It is interesting to note, however, that Schuller and Burns (1999) identify this kind of 'foregoing of self interest' (p.58) as illustrative of the kind of community cohesion desirable for lifelong learning. The fact that these values did not materialise into high adult participation rates raises questions about what other power dynamics were operating. Indeed, most of the women recalled some form of attitudinal restriction regarding their education, summed up by Muriel as follows: 'In my day parents didn't often think that girls needed the same sort of education as boys'.

The idea of extended learning 'not mattering' (for class or gender reasons) seemed to be irrefutable common sense - in the same way that 'appropriateness' was used in the academic discussions regarding curriculum development. A closer look at the participants' educational experiences revealed, however, a number of inconsistencies between the way those expectations were portrayed then and now. There was, for instance, a common educational argument for leaving school as soon as possible: 'You'd get a job easily enough, yeah it wasn't difficult' (Margaret age 56). In spite of the apparent availability of jobs, however, the reality of options, especially for girls, was 'very limited' (Peggy, age 54) to factory or shop work, with the possibility of office work if you had attended certain schools in the A stream: 'If you were in an A class, well then you were encouraged to further your education [to do secretarial subjects]' (Emma, age 53). In these reflections, then, the discourse of 'plenty' had reinscribed the notion of 'limitation'. The inconsistency between these truths is submerged however because the discourses were being used by all sectors of society. This had the effect of reinforcing certain expectations and inhibiting a search for other options (disciplinary power).

Such colluding partnerships, between those with and without authority to know, had similar effects on perceptions of who goes to university. A consistent message from all of the participants was that you had to be extremely clever or have money to go to university: 'Working class people didn't go to university it was only people with money, that was the image when I was a girl anyway' (Peggy); 'People who entered universities, they're talking about very clever people, you know, ... and people who can afford to go there' (Chris). Even if you were clever, the prospect of a university education for working class children would still be remote. For some this reflected the hardships of the time, as stated by Muriel: 'If they were ordinary working class people they struggled very very hard to put their children through university' (age 62).

But now they were adults, some simply found new rationales for not participating. They still hung to the principle of cleverness but made it fit today's slightly more affluent circumstances. For instance, Emma justified the ability of working class children to get to university now because: 'Young people today seem to be a lot more intelligent than we were'. The implication of this statement therefore was that the older working class generation (and therefore herself) simply did not have the ability. This discourse placed the burden of failure within her own social class rather than the dominant class. Whilst not everyone offered Emma's explanation there were examples of similarly inconsistent ways of presenting arguments which justified the younger generation's right and accessibility to a university education. Julie, for instance, associated the changing economic climate with the need to get qualifications:

I have encouraged them to get as much education following on from school as they could um because things are different now, I feel you need more

79

qualifications if you're gonna try and get any sort of decent work ... I think they probably have more of a cross-section of people now [at university] (Julie, age 44).

The significance of these statements is in the way new arguments are constructed. To Julie it appeared that things are different now and this is the reason why working class people need - and get - more education. Volman and ten Dam (1998) suggest that this kind of contradictory discourse is having a similar effect on current day perceptions of equal opportunities practice. They state that assumed equal opportunities practices belie the reality and stop people looking for and challenging inequalities. Even the perceived increased participation in higher education amongst working class children is not statistically born out in proportion to participation across the social classes. Indeed class differentials in participation rates have barely changed for two generations (Dearing 1997). Equally, the reality that working class children usually needed qualifications in the past to get 'decent work' is ignored in the new discourse which claims new needs for changing industrial work patterns.

The issue here is one of power. The dominant argument of the 1950s and 1960s was that either working class children didn't have the ability or work was so plentiful that there was no need to seek different options (Roberts 1995). The changing economic climate in the 1980s and 1990s presents new arguments that working class children are more able and in need of qualifications because jobs are scarce. What has been ignored are the isolated struggles of individuals who did try to obtain qualifications in a political climate which previously had no economic need - and therefore no desire - to make education available.

Chris's story illustrates this point. He had followed his father's footsteps into the steel making trade - a job which he loved and of which he was proud. When the opportunity to train for electric steel making arrived Chris volunteered. He capitalised on this opportunity through private reading and talking to more experienced colleagues. Although this was a vocationally linked initiative, it was Chris's personal interest in metallurgy which drove him to study beyond what was required for the job. Indeed he said if there had been a local opportunity to study metallurgy, one which also accommodated his shift work, he would have taken it. This is one of several individual stories across the Portside learners which will be discussed later. Many revealed unsupported attempts at further study in a climate which had claimed that education was not necessary, in order to suppress demand. There is evidence, however, from research relating to the 1980s that:

Although relatively few adults recorded themselves as participants in adult education in the formal sense, many were actively engaged in organised learning projects (Schuller & Bostyn 1993: 367).

Truth, then, is a construction to suit the dominant power holders. The paradox of an assumed current day change, rather than continuation, of interest for working class children is revealed in the new learning discourse of the 1990s. The implied portrayal, for instance, of the new higher education as more vocational and instrumental is that this focus is a necessary incentive for the new generation of working class learners. There are indications, however, that even this discourse is not winning over the hearts and minds of present day working class men (McGivney 1999). Yet higher education for the middle classes, and amongst the academic comments in earlier chapters, was valued primarily for its personal development qualities. Equally the working class incentive to study on these community courses had more to do with a sense of personal interest rather than vocational goals per se:

> I were just eager to, you know find out you know things that were perhaps I was lacking in because when I started me family history it was just a case of er floundering in the dark (Peggy, age 54).

Foucault sought to expose inconsistencies in history which give an appearance of continuity or reason. One contradiction in these discourses is the way higher education was portrayed as of intrinsic value for the middle class individual alongside the more recent notion that higher education is simply a necessary vocational requisite for the working classes. History claims changing economic circumstances as a reason for encouraging increased participation in education from a disinterested workforce. Yet the history of the dominant social structure constructs 'regimes of truth' about cleverness, job availability, learning value and learner entitlement. It is only when different discourses are juxtaposed that the fragility of those truths are exposed.

These conflicting truths stretched across all the learner groups. An additional factor for the Wyrevale learners was their varying stages of disability onset. This added other kinds of reality as the participants described how they had to contend with disability discourses as well as class issues.

Wyrevale

Three of the learners at Wyrevale had attended but not completed college courses prior to the university's involvement. Seven in all attended more than one university community course. With the exception of Tony who claimed an apprenticeship in the textile industry and Henry who had owned a farm, most had undertaken unskilled manual jobs throughout their working lives. Apart from Henry's well connected Methodist family parents of the other participants also had manual and labouring jobs. The two disabled tutors, Lesley and Mavis, had middle class backgrounds.

Paul and Gillian who had some form of physical disability from birth and one tutor, Mavis, who acquired hers in early childhood, recalled hospitalised periods of time off school. The second tutor, Lesley, acquired a progressive disability as a young adult.

The onset of disability had resulted in disrupted career plans or work expectations for everyone. None obtained any school qualifications and only Carol knew universities offered courses for adults, though two had children who studied beyond A level. Almost all of them remembered low school expectations, except Henry who was privately educated. In contrast to Portside only five participants were married at the time of the courses. These findings confirm a range of literature which asserts the low academic expectations for working class children. But for disabled children, these expectations were reinforced in special schools and most disabled children were expected to be unemployable (Oliver 1996, Barnes 1991, Fish 1992). Fine and Asch (1981) and Clark and Hirst (1989) also highlight the decreased possibility of marriage and family prospects amongst people with disabilities. The Wyrevale group therefore met Clayton's description of social exclusion in terms of their: 'exclusion from participating in normal social and economic life of the community' (1999: 13). Indeed Morris (1991) points out that the segregation of disabled people from mainstream society: 'is an important part of the material experience of powerlessness' (p. 117). In contradistinction to this enforced reality Hurst (1990: 113) emphasises the extra need for disabled people, as a population, to have qualifications as a 'key to a steady job'.

As only a minority were disabled as children other considerations for their exclusion needed to be taken into account as well. For instance, nearly all participants talked of unsatisfactory school experiences: 'There wasn't a teacher who wanted to teach yer' (Tony, age 55). Many recalled unhappy childhood and adult relationships, covering violence, bullying, neglect and religious discrimination, which according to Oppenheim (1998) and Schuller (1998) would delimit their access to social capital. There was no

82

simple explanation to their current shared situation, however. Henry and Gillian, for example, described happy, caring childhoods.

In other ways the Wyrevale group's educational expectations usually followed the working class memories from Portside:

> It wouldn't have mattered anyway because even if you passed your eleven plus in them days our generation sort of thing you just left school at fifteen ... and you either went to work in a shop or a factory or anywhere where you were earning some money (Mandy, age 45).

In the working class authorised truths for the fifties and sixties jobs were plentiful: 'If you didn't fancy what you were doing you'd say go home Friday night you could finish and on the Monday morning go to another job, that's how good it was' (Tony). Qualifications were neither necessary nor offered; and 'work' usually meant manual labour. While many middle class families did not extend their academic qualifications through formal education, however, Henry (age 56) confirmed a different set of options for his privately educated peers:

> When they got to the sixteen age group they left to go into their father's business or erm into somewhere they knew, into banking or into a solicitor's or something like that.

The participants' disability realities would nevertheless reveal a range of contradictions for both middle and working classes. For instance, in spite of a popular historical picture of full employment Gillian, whose cerebral palsy affected her walking, took two years to find a factory job on leaving school: 'It took ages - till I was eighteen years of age ... I went down the employment exchange ... I never got any money cause I was handicapped' (age 48). Even middle class Mavis was denied the opportunity to train for her chosen teaching career:

> I wanted to teach in a junior school ... and they said that I wouldn't be able to maintain discipline from a seated [wheelchair] position ... I mean it wouldn't happen now but er it did happen and at seventeen you just accept that, that's what people told you and that avenue's not an option anymore (age 48).

Mavis also took two years to find a job. Paul and Gillian's special schools did not even have working class goals in mind: 'I think with the special school a lot of the er staff thought that when people left the school that would be it they'd just do nothing with their lives' (Paul, age 37). Even

83

Carol, with access to the qualification system of the time, was only seen by those with authority to know in disability terms (Slack 1999). Although she did obtain a job, she was denied the option of staying on to do O levels because her writing arm was 'getting worse': 'The headmaster and the er governors they wrote to the em doctor and he decided, you know' (age 51).

These memories not only revealed working class truths but they also exposed disability realities which excluded them from the very systems which could have facilitated the kind of social integration advocated by Howarth & Kenway (1998) for social inclusion. In view of Carol's and Mavis's grammar school education this picture also confirms Lloyd's (1992) claim that women with disabilities, of whatever class, were not expected to obtain skilled work. On occasions when ability seemed to contradict the expected normality of 'disability', professionals colluded to re-establish the expected norm (Fish 1992, Abberley 1987, Swain and Cameron 1999).

For each of the other participants the job market predictably closed at the onset of adulthood disability. Only a few noticed, however, the discourses of an education system which both discouraged educational qualifications for working class children generally and subsequently contributed to the Wyrevale group's present state of unemployment. Tutor Mavis pointed out the incoherence of a world which portrays the labour market in terms which simply exclude disability experiences - thereby silencing awareness of their needs:

> You could earn a living as unskilled as long as you're fit and able bodied but once you've acquired a disability that door is no longer open to you so you can't translate your work into office work or something that is easy to do from a point of disability. So you get back to the basic education problem ...they've had no opportunity ... to develop new skills ... nothing's been offered since they became disabled, the system doesn't seek them out.

Indeed while unemployment itself is often described as a 'disabling experience' (Dadzie 1990: 33), the desirable connection between disability, education and work is seldom made. As Room (1995) states:

> Where citizens are unable to secure their social rights, they will tend to suffer processes of generalised and persisting disadvantage and their social and occupational participation will be undermined (p 7).

The learners' comments demonstrate the contradictory nature of historical records of employment and educational opportunities when

84

compared with disability realities. They also show how certain ways of seeing the world are simply reproduced over time. Individuals need considerable strength if they are to off-load the image imposed on them by others. Those who had some cultural capital were more successful, but still at a personal cost: 'It's just painful and time consuming and sometimes you feel like you might give in but you mustn't' (Lesley, age 53).

History, then produces one form of truth. The nuances of 'other' voices are consequently not well represented in literature on participation - especially if you are disabled: 'To have a disability is to be reinscribed as other' (Marks 1994: 83). The next chapter shows how people often failed to get beyond the dominant images which were imposed on them. Later chapters, however, show that some individuals were able to create their own sense of agency and their own rationalities in spite of everything.

The stories from Wyrevale and Portside were about two kinds of working class experiences; those who obtained apprenticeships and relatively stable work patterns and those whose fragmented employment relied entirely on unskilled work. Their individual stories revealed the silences in history as well as shared 'truths' about class and education constructed through the dominant Western middle class discourse. The stories of the younger Loamshire women revealed yet another mixture of intergenerational realities amidst very different cultures and with their own dominant discourses. These stories both challenge and reinforce dominant images of social exclusion.

Loamshire

The complications of attaching social class labels to ethnic minority communities in England has been acknowledged (Bourke 1994, Hannan 1987). For instance, the educational backgrounds and family connections of several participants, indicated they were middle class. Shila came from a family of teachers, Sara's father was a solicitor, Shivani's father was a police inspector. According to their postcode the Loamshire women all lived in working class areas (THES 1997). Many also married husbands whose qualifications and work roles matched those of the Portside and Wyrevale groups, though there were some exceptions. Three husbands, for instance, held professional jobs in this country. Social class for many Asian families in England therefore was complex. People's social mobility was affected by migration; work acquired in England did not necessarily match that of the home country (Bhachu 1993). An additional factor for this group was their ethnicity, defined here by their country of origin. Ethnic identity and adjustment to new cultures is also a complex and fluid process where ethnicity definitions are equally as complicated as those of social class, particularly for generations born as minorities in their host country (Woollett et al 1994, Kassam 1997). These factors alone placed the women within Oppenheim's definition of social exclusion by virtue of their being 'detached from the [dominant] organisations and communities of which the society is composed and from the rights and obligations that they embody' (1998: 13).

This group was much younger than the other two groups. Nine of the women were in their twenties while the remaining four were in their early thirties. All participants were married though two tutors, Amita and Afsar, were divorced. Of the three tutors who contributed to this study, Kajal admitted to being working class according to her father's occupation and Afsar middle class. Nearly all the women had attended other community courses prior to the university's involvement. In Loamshire X these were solely ESOL classes. In Loamshire Y three women had taken advantage of the HCC's wide range of training contacts. They participated in office skills, as well as courses such as henna painting. Adult education, then, was already perceived by the participants as something they did a lot of, though most would register as 'non participants' in formal education terms and were, therefore, already invisible.

None of the women were working at the beginning of the study though one Pakistani woman, Sanam, and Madhun in Loamshire Y had worked before marriage in their homelands. Three of the Indian women (Shivani, Vijayanti and Shila) worked in factories on arrival in England irrespective of their Indian qualifications.

Eight out of the ten participants' husbands had been educated in England. Of the Pakistani educated men, Hinaa's was in prison and Ruksana's had never been to school. The Loamshire participants included women who were both the most and least qualified of all the participants described in this book. Even so, with the exception of Afsar and Madhun, marriage interrupted everyone's education. Most were sad their education, and in some cases, career ambitions had been disrupted, but all accepted the inevitability of marriage, in line with current literature on the subject (Episto 1994, Afshar 1994). Shila even stated she had been 'ready to get married' in spite of its disruption to her studies. Two, plus the tutor Kajal, admitted to having unhappy marriages. All four Hindu women had ambitions to teach or work in administration or commerce.

Although most were married at a young age, there was usually a link between year of marriage, age and qualifications achieved. Those married most recently, were also marrying at an older age, after a longer period in full time education, and with more likelihood of work experience - reflecting their expressed pace of change in Pakistan and India in the last few years.

All were educated at single sex schools from the age of 10 and at least five continued their studies beyond O levels in a single sex college before marriage. Teaching styles in Pakistan and India were consistently recorded as more formal than their experiences here; many made detailed comparisons about the gains and disadvantages of each system. None realised that universities offered short courses for adults and most expected university study to mean postgraduate level learning. It was all the more significant, then, that seven identified relatives who had been to university. This level of educational expectation was unmatched by the other groups. Furthermore, perhaps because of their backgrounds, or simply influenced by the need to learn English, all ten women mentioned some form of additional study in the home. This was usually through watching TV and reading obtained from their own children or the library. TV education is still a strategy which seems relatively unexploited by the media or education professions (Fryer 1997).

All ten women stated that they had been actively encouraged by their school and family to study as children - and most cited the influence of their fathers even during long periods of family separation. Neither education nor work, however, were expected beyond marriage for most of the Muslim women. The extent to which discourses are changing towards work, education and marriage for women is reflected in the education and career expectations of the youngest Indian Sub Continent participants and the youngest tutor. In contrast, tutors Kajal and Amita, both in their thirties, fought against family opposition to gain qualifications as mature students. Mirza (1997) confirms that a common strategy to obtain higher education amongst Asian women would be to take an acceptably gendered work role as a 'back door' route into study. Kajal and Amita initially followed this practice by obtaining jobs in the health services as bilingual link workers. Their efforts bear some resemblance to the struggles of Peggy and Mavis in the other interview groups. In contrast, Afsar, in her early 20s when she taught on the community courses, had received no opposition to study from her parents.

In this country most participants' attempts to study further were often interrupted by family commitments or return trips to the homeland. Amongst these participants there was a sense that the UK and the Indian Sub Continent are highly interchangeable for people of Asian heritage. Family ties are strong and visits abroad can turn into residential stays of several years for children and adults. All these differences of generation, space and culture will be explored in more detail in the following chapters.

One particular example of the relationship between culture and geographical space was when one tutor, Afsar, described the women's first reactions to their arrival in England. She explained how culture shock pervades the whole infrastructure of a person's values, way of life and even physical use of space. Truth for Pakistani and Indian women on arrival in England had to undergo reconstruction from the moment they set foot on its ground:

> You always find one fixed term that everybody says when they come from Pakistan about England and it's always: 'This country's like a prison' and they always use the word prison, because the houses are closed, so you look at the country physically, the first impression you get - you know, closed rooftops, closed, walled houses, you never find that in Pakistan. You have open gardens, right you have flat roofs and you have people sitting on roofs and walking about, so you will always find people on tops of houses, the gardens are open, the walls might be high, but the whole place is open. You don't find that here, everything is so enclosed (age 23).

In this description, place and space in the Indian Subcontinent had a sense of openness, irrespective of what appear to Westerners to be restrictive lives for Asian women. For example:

> In Pakistan, India and Bangladesh, rural women have their responsibilities and a physical terrain which is theirs to control. In England the reality is of marginalisation (Ali 1992: 112).

The women's traditional space and sense of place became colonised and transformed in the UK climate so that some only felt their restriction in England. Meanings, then, had separate and separating values for the whole infrastructure of society and its different generations.

In Foucault's Genealogy of Knowledge (1972) he revealed seemingly contradictory events which are sifted out and silenced by the dominant voice to give the impression of continuity and a particular kind of reality over time. As a white Westerner looking into the dominant discourses of Asian cultures I followed a process of sometimes conflicting discourses between older families already settled in England and new arrivals from the modern generation of Pakistan and India (see also Hartley 1994). These differences seemed to exemplify Foucault's genealogical perspective.

Furthermore, Western notions of freedom would appear to have strange and unconnected meanings for some of the women. In many cases Islam was regarded as a form of liberation from Western racisms and also a discourse through which women could negotiate their rights within the family and community (Brettel & Simon 1986, Westwood & Bhachu 1988, Young 1994, Saghal & Yuval Davis 1992, Jacobson 1997). However, where earlier generations, trapped in location time warps, might encourage conservative attitudes to women's space, their space in this country could result in being totally hidden. Sanam, for instance, was restricted by her prison-like living environment as well as the attitudes of her in-laws (see also Afshar 1994a), who refused to let her out of the house while she lived with them:

> I come from a very liberated family. I can't believe I am so limited in what I can do in England. I was so liberated in Pakistan in so many ways. I can't believe that I have been so restricted here by my in-laws. When I first came here I said 'is this what you all call Great Britain, which is supposed to be so free?' (Sanam).

The first generation practices of Asian settlements in the UK would also impinge on the new lifestyle of more recent arrivals, making events which seemed logical to one generation appear contradictory to the other (Bhachu 1991). Tutor Amita explained why:

> In India and Pakistan things have moved on; now the people who came from those countries thirty years ago they still hold the same values of twenty / thirty years ago. What has happened in India has moved on; the country, the people of Pakistan and India they have moved on. They don't have the same values as those people who came over twenty or thirty years ago, but these people think they have and they are holding onto it (age 33).

The women's attitudes to their marriage, education and their in-laws depended on which generational values were predominant. Discourse positions also depended on how they interfaced with the dominant attitudes of their host region. This experience is confirmed by many writers, such as Yuval Davis (1992), Woollett et al (1994), Bakare-Yusef (1997). Ali (1992) and others point out that this part of England is a particularly complicated terrain for Asian women as their lives also intermesh with regional gender attitudes towards women. Aliya (age 33), for instance, arrived in 1975 into a conservative, North-England environment. Local Western attitudes towards women reinforced the status quo amongst Asian communities. So the self regulation of traditional principles underpinned her home-based family role in the extended family of her in-laws. She felt she 'was not restricted in any way' and was proud of 'the way I treat my in-laws'. In different parts of the country there was a different mixture of dominant discourses. In some cases new and old would harmonise with regard to education and training. Then traditional cultural values for such things as extended family relations would be welcomed by the modern, educated and outgoing bride (Brettell & Simon 1986, Bhachu 1986). So Madhun, one of the newest arrivals, into a different part of Loamshire (Loamshire Y), was able to build on her degree acquired in India and the opportunities of living and working in her new environment:

> Here my husband, my in-laws, you know there's no problem. ...They like me to improve my skills, to be able to talk on my own. I have to get to know the system here ... they would like me to progress. They don't mind, my in-laws don't mind me going to [place] or other areas, you know so long as I'm .. familiar with all the roads and the buses (age 24).

Sanam, in contrast, arrived at Loamshire X in 1987 - but from a well-educated background and experience of work in Pakistan:

> I was leading such a free life in Pakistan and I was earning; I had so much money coming in, I could spend it or do whatever I wanted to and I came here and I felt so trapped and I felt well everybody thinks I'm coming to England - I'm going to live in a nice modern country and I hated it here when I first came. In fact I still don't like it because my living standard isn't nice (age 25).

The women would have to accommodate vastly different truths embedded in each country's culture. To understand fully the implications, and starkness, of their contrasting experiences it is necessary to hear the women's own stories of their lives from the homeland. Depending on their age, geographical location and class background, these stories highlight extreme differences and changes in educational opportunity, especially for women (Kandiyoti 1991). Being 'educated', for example, could mean something very different from current Western discourses, as Ruksana demonstrated when she discussed her education which finished at the age of nine in a small rural village:

> Well education is valued but not so much in schools. It wasn't always in the school environment. It was more so continuing at home ... more than education in school we were emphasised to go towards Islamic education (age 23).

Values about providing a solely religious education for girls were changing to a concern for more academic study. But these changes seemed to depend on when schooling became more widely available for girls; that is within the dominant discourse which says that girls should not travel far to school. Hinaa, for instance, stayed at school till she was eighteen because of the availability of single sex provision. In her village schooling was the norm:

> Everybody went to school whether you were girls or boys - our school was actually just a girls school and it was a high school so it was all the way to matriculation [O levels], whereas the boys had a primary school and after the age of nine they had to go to a separate town for their school (age 20).

Whilst many discussed the changes and technological advances in their country of origin, it was only Kajal who pointed out how relatively recently education changes had taken place in this country - both in schools and for adults. Dominant discourses have a habit of making certain truths appear the norm very quickly:

> Well I've been in this country, what nearly 27 years now and I can see a great change in women's attitudes towards education and before I mean there was this like textile factories and that and nobody bothered to go back and do it because there was a lot of work and people just wanted to carry on and make money and you know have a better life but nowadays with the jobs being so scarce and lots of opportunities available now, within ... five years ... really and there is more and more emphasis on education and training because before when you spoke of going to college and that they thought you were crazy ... I can see a lot of change now.

The intersection of these changing economic and political forces and their influence on educational decision making in Britain is also confirmed in the literature (for example, Bhachu 1991).

The interface of so many discourses had a range of effects on the creation of new truths in the new living situations. Cultural attitudes which may have been less noticeable in the homeland appeared to rise almost in opposition to each other as new power struggles took place in the UK. In other cases, women enjoyed new freedoms and opportunities so that: 'We re-locate ourselves in the present historical moment by reconfiguring our identities relatively' (Bhavnani & Haraway 1994: 21). In spite of, or perhaps because of, all these fragile relations in the new reality, some of the women were reluctant to adopt values which were clearly Western. As a result they were caught in a double power struggle of male domination from the East and cultural resistance to Western domination (Bakare-Yusef 1997).

One example of this struggle concerned the notion of higher education. For Aliya her truth constructed higher education as a corrupting Western influence which will lead women astray from morality and into prostitution (Afshar 1989). Aliya offered a complex interpretation of 'rights' and 'immorality' in her defence of the dominant truth as she knew it:

> People like me who are not very educated say that the only reason why girls demand their rights and go off and do things they are not supposed to do is because they have gone away from home and they have studied.

Again, with hints of nineteenth century England (Purvis 1991), some of the older women would accept the inevitability of women not going away to university, and live with the truth of those statements as a form of 'disciplinary power' (self surveillance). Unfortunately Western lifestyles exacerbate such power struggles. In a climate of two very different cultures where the host country fails to respect even the religious practices of such things as alcohol free social habits and single sex learning zones, and differing views of geographical space, then the thoughts from new generations of women caught between the two worlds appear threatening or inappropriate (Bhachu 1993). All these issues would affect how education should be made available to the course participants. Indeed the positive experiences of the community courses meant that some people would now view the possibility of university study differently:

> I would now say; they are not just high level courses, adult courses are run for those who don't have much knowledge and I'd give my welfare rights course as an example (Sara).

This chapter has used Foucault's perspective of 'historicity' (1972) to demonstrate that truth and reality are contingent and ephemeral. Whilst some new truths can be created relatively quickly, others are re-rationalised to justify old power positions, resulting in the continued exclusion of certain individuals. Dominant educational discourses have the effect of silencing some people unless attention is paid to the cracks in-between what is 'normal'. The extent to which people collude in and are dominated by discourses which silence issues of race, gender, disability, class or culture will be discussed in chapter seven. Chapters eight and nine, however, show that these positions are not static. Many individuals struggled to create alternative identities for themselves from the prescribed norm. The opportunity to understand such constraints and opportunities broadens our understanding of how to develop education provision which is meaningful and inclusive.

7   The creation of social exclusion

> You begin to realise actually how many people patronise and how many people think you are sort of, not quite up to scratch. I don't know whether you ever noticed, perhaps you haven't, but some people's voice changes when they talk to people with disabilities. You know the way people's voice changes when they talk to children ... I mean you get used to that and you get to think well it must be true (Lesley, Wyrevale tutor).

Slack (1999) and Swain and Cameron (1999) have recently discussed how disabled people struggle not just with the actuality of their impairment, but also the labels and consequent behaviours people attribute to them under the representation of 'disabled'. This process of externally referenced representation applies to all minority groups of course. The personal, insider perspectives of class, gender, race, disability are either regarded as deviant or silenced out by the dominant, middle class, white and able bodied view of the world. For people born into the most dominant of social fields - cultural capital (naturalised superiority) - there are several mechanisms in place (discourses) which safeguard this dominant balance of power. So professionals, employers, family - people who make up the social framework of society - act unconsciously as 'agents' of power. They measure difference against the dominant, internalised norm. Their dominance is subtle, however. For instance, agents of power may express political agendas on behalf of difference through a discourse of care (pastoral power). The effectiveness of these various roles can be measured by the extent to which people absorb the meaning of those discourses. Society's harmony is most effective when people monitor or control their own behaviour or thoughts (disciplinary power). Then people who are not members of society's elite - those without cultural capital in Western society - collude in their own social exclusion. This process means that ultimately you provide your own rationalities for maintaining the image that others have already imposed on you.

People's lives were not totally manipulated of course and dominant attitudes were resisted. But to show how difficult such resistance was, this chapter looks at the cumulative impact on people's lives of the interlinked network of agencies which often speak in frightening unison when it comes to social exclusion. From the outset the attitudes of friends, family and professionals impinged on the community participants' own educational decision making, with consequences for their whole lives.

Some readers may think that there is little need to concern ourselves with the memories of an older generation because times appear to have changed so much. Comments across the various generations show, however, that where specific barriers may seem to diminish, others take their place, ensuring a continuity of exclusion. So even if some of these examples are already recorded as part of a bygone era (for example, Roberts 1995, Jackson and Marsden 1973), my argument remains: people re-rationalise their discourses for exclusion in different and subtle ways. It is only by understanding our shared responsibility in perpetuating certain power relationships that we can hope to do something about them.

Attitudes of the past affected personal expectations in the present. The participants would find employment or education seeking experiences reinforcing old expectations with the result that personal ambitions would be re-constructed to suit the dominant view of them as a woman, disabled or whatever. Then, even when opportunities seemed to be more flexible, the participants themselves would unconsciously construct new rationales for self exclusion. Perpetuating old patterns, they would set their ambitions apart from the apparent flexibility of the present. Each of those phases will be looked at separately here.

Attitudes of the past

> Where citizens are unable to secure their social rights they will tend to suffer processes of generalised and persisting disadvantage and their social and occupational participation will be undermined (Room 1995: 7).

Whilst the discourse of social exclusion attempts to avoid 'blaming the victim' (Brine 1999, Clayton 1999) it does not sufficiently accept responsibility for causing the situation in the first place. The following (and indeed earlier) examples demonstrate that exclusion is not only cumulative, it is also perpetuated within the very infrastructure of society and its wider discourses.

Peggy had lost her mother as a baby and experienced frequent time off school as a child. She eventually passed the thirteen plus but there were no places at the grammar school, a situation which she always regretted.

Alongside these setbacks she absorbed her working class parents' educational expectations for girls:

> Me dad was a Victorian, he was born in 1899. In his day it was a case of getting a job, going out to work ... No matter what education you had you took your brains with you down the nearest mine. Step mothers' views were, well girls only get married anyway ... you pick up other people's attitudes don't you? So if ... education's not important, that's what the two people closest to me thought, so I thought the same (Peggy).

Even Muriel, who felt well supported at home, was not allowed to sit the eleven plus exam. She was still expected to leave at 14 and was actively encouraged in her search for a job: 'My mother took me round to different places to see if there was a job available'. Muriel had an unusually good job for a woman as a confectioner apprentice. Nevertheless these were the heights she was expected to aim for: 'If you were working class you didn't very often have expectations'. The resultant effect of these attitudes was a form of self surveillance - as Julie indicated:

> Well there was nothing really that I felt I wanted to do you know. I left school, I got a job, I was quite happy to sort of tick over. I was never very ambitious ... I didn't feel I needed any more education or training.

Several people talked of how the school curriculum 'moulded' people for their future role. Sheila, for instance reported how her school curriculum 'educated you to be a housewife and mother'. Parents generally colluded in this by supporting the goal to leave school and earn money. This was partly because of the perceived immediate family benefits of this option (Mac an Ghaill 1994, Roberts 1995). Muriel, Sheila, Graham and Eric all reported parental help over securing their first job. In addition, Eric received further, work-related educational encouragement from his father and Muriel's parents encouraged her to go to night school. But parents generally felt their children had already received a better education than them. Full time education was encouraged only up to the legally required age. Neither school nor parents - nor industry, expected any more than vocational learning, even when grammar education was available. Indeed Graham intimated that the firm P_____ preferred Tec boys because their training was more suited to the industry's job requirements and, by implication, the curriculum was one which encouraged gender-specific ways of knowing. These expectations seem to have barely shifted across generations. Graham, for instance felt no more pressure to educate himself beyond the prospect of P_____, or a trade, than his older contemporaries. Similarly Sheila and Julie confirmed their parents just wanted them to be happy.

The Wyrevale group's choice of career or learning routes were also determined by their experiences of colluding discourses. Dave acquired most of his belief systems from school and family experiences of a rough and male dominated 'pit village' environment. Unlike the Portside cohort, however, who were encouraged to undertake apprenticeships, Dave chose to remain a labourer in the building trade, providing his own rationale for doing so: 'If you were an apprentice you went on an apprenticeship salary which were a damn sight lower and you couldn't do any over time'. The Portside men confirmed this issue, but none considered this was a reason for not doing an apprenticeship. Why, then, did Dave find this an unacceptable goal for himself? We can only compare Dave's home and school discourses and experiences with those of, say, Graham, Chris and Eric. Unlike the Portside people, Dave had no parental support for his education or personal development. His mother was dead and his father responded in most cases violently to Dave's behaviour. Money was an issue for all the men, but for Dave its significance started at school when he learnt to steal to offset the bullying tactics of his peers to take his dinner money and, later, to secure peer friendship by sharing cigarettes. The goal of his approved school was to get him any kind of job, rather than a career. So, for Dave, employment had different meanings and power relationships with others from the Portside interviews. The effect of those discourses, however, would be long lasting.

The Loamshire women revealed similarly ambivalent attitudes towards schooling. Nine out of the ten learners confirmed they had received positive encouragement about their education from parents and teachers; in particular their fathers. Indeed at first it seems the Loamshire women had a more social capital and a more consistently positive view of the importance of education for themselves than the Wyrevale and Portside groups. Foucault's notion of 'agency', however, represents the intention of power. Encouragement, as for the other two groups, had its constraints. For these women the constraints centred round their cultural role as girls, local circumstances and their future role as wives (Saghal & Yuval Davis 1992). The Loamshire women rarely saw these discourses as oppression. Sabia, for instance, with echoes of Gladys' fatalism from Portside, simply said: 'It's the Pakistani way of life, you have to accept that'. As chapter six showed, schooling was encouraged but in direct proportion to its compliance with cultural demands - such as single sex schooling and marriage arrangements.

There followed, from these early memories of what was expected of them, a pattern of self-fulfilling goals amongst the learners.

Resultant expectations for self

In keeping with Roberts (1995) observations of Northern working class women born in the forties and fifties, all the women in Portside seemed happy to be housewives and mothers: 'that was my role and I was happy with it' (Gladys). In keeping with their internalised acceptance of the school curriculum, they each assigned themselves responsibilities which categorised them as carers and servers. So, for instance, the women saw looking after elderly parents and in-laws as a demanding, but common sense given (Roberts 1995). Education was seen as a 'tie' which might interfere with other demands. The tie of parents or in-laws, however, was reinscribed as a commitment: 'I've now got me mum whose ninety one living with me ... I have to give quite a bit of time to her ... it wouldn't always be easy to do homework' (Muriel).

Some of the Loamshire women responded in similar fashion - particularly those from Loamshire X. Saghal and Yuval-Davis (1992) explain that in England power relations intersect with the effects of racism as well as patriarchy, so that the need for community cohesion creates: 'strong ties that bind women to communities which in other ways frustrate their aspirations' (p. 106). For Pakistani and Muslim women, these assumed constraints were conditioned by their own tradition of extended family responsibilities (Afshar 1994). The women's desire to conform to in-law expectations was therefore as strong for new arrivals like Madhun and Shila as for older generations like Sara and Aliya. Aliya's terminology was significant: 'My parents are so happy with the way I treat my in-laws and that I show them respect and love and I do, I really do feel a lot for my in-laws'. Aliya's concept of success was described entirely in terms of how *she* was responding to her in-laws, rather than indications of mutuality. The desire to conform and do what is right was second nature to Aliya and consisted of taking on the gender role of care and obedience as well as being custodian of religious beliefs (Afshar 1994a). Ruksana's comment, too, was typical and closely echoed the Portside women: 'I like the way I spend my time. I have children to look after. I'm obviously kept busy working so it's cooking and cleaning etc'. Similarly, like Muriel from Portside, Shivani, Madhun and Shila all took on an assumed commitment to family responsibilities: 'Now I'm married I've got a husband I've got a mother-in-law, I've got a father-in-law, so I've got to think about them as well before I do anything' (Shivani).

We see later, however, that the Loamshire women's acceptance of their situation also mingled with dominant views from their immediate locality. Sanam, Afsar, Kajal, Amita, Vijayanti all revealed different struggles. Equally we shall see, in Madhun, Shivani and Shila, a new disciplinary power relationship with in-laws and husbands which not only kept them within their modern Asian culture but also gave them different expectations for themselves as women, compared with earlier generations.

The discourse of care is a bit like the discourse of appropriateness which I mentioned in chapters four and five. Women carers were assigned a positive status to prevent them looking beyond the role of carer. This produced an unproblematic notion of care as something positive and unchallengeable. This perception facilitated its use as a form of pastoral power by the dominant, acting upon the dominated. The assumed positive meaning of care meant its discourse would be unchallenged, irrespective of the outcome. This was never more evident than amongst those who had a disability.

The discourse of care

All the Wyrevale participants cited disability related instances of oppression which affected every aspect of their lives. But oppression was often disguised in the professional discourse of 'care' (Corbett 1990). Henry recalled, for example, his first attempt at mobility independence during a visit to hospital shortly after his stroke. He wanted to walk, rather than be wheelchaired to the ambulance:

I got up and one of the nurses shouted at me in a guttural voice: 'Where do you think you're going?' .. And she said: 'Sit down!' ... they were frightened of me falling you see.

A series of well meaning professional interventions were made throughout Carol's schooling and adulthood, which ultimately disempowered her from any sense of personal agency. The decision for her to leave the grammar school was legitimated in the context of her disability and assumed working class expectations, in spite of her original desire to become a nurse: 'They said if I had a job to go to it was really pointless to take the exams because there wasn't the pressure on people [to get qualifications]'. These experiences confirm Swain's (1993) contention that

99

disabled children rarely have any say in their education as they are simply: 'passed from the hands of one professional to another' (p. 157). As Carol herself had absorbed the inevitability that her condition would not be accepted for a nursing career, the logic was secure and uncontested without reconsideration of other equivalent work options: 'I knew I wasn't steady enough for nursing so I took the next job like, you know - in a wool shop'. Things did not stop there however. Both employers and the medical profession ultimately succeeded in excluding Carol from the employment market altogether. After 18 years of working in the wool shop, it was taken over by new management who put pressure on Carol to work faster and use a new till. When Carol turned to her doctor for support the medical model of depression then 'cared' for her with drugs. The doctors simply compounded her difficulty by slowing her down: 'You see, they gave me anti-depressants, which didn't really work. I think they made me, you know, drugged me'. She eventually became ill and was sacked.

Agents of disability discourses included teachers, family members, peers, doctors, social services, probation and employers. The colluding effect of these agency attitudes to disability, education and class was demonstrated in different ways. For Gillian, it was her parents who elected that she should stay in special school, even when a mainstream alternative was offered her as a teenager:

> They thought with me being 14 and a half ... that with me to have a basic education which is what they thought I had, that I might be put with the young kids.

Gillian's parents colluded with the discourse of the time which designated disability as fragile and in need of prolonged parenting (Barnes 1993, Chapman 1990): 'They always used to treat me like a wee kiddie, you know, like: "Come on here then love, come on darling"'.

There were other examples. In Loamshire, for instance, parents would also use a discourse of care to argue against a university education. Ruksana said:

> My parents were afraid that if I were to get into the town then they would lose ties with me and they feared that I'd adopt more of a Western way of life, rather than an Eastern way and I'd probably go out and I don't know perhaps indulge in activities that they wouldn't be very pleased about.

Similarly, arguments to prevent women working were used by in-laws with the same apparent protectiveness (Ali 1992). Ruksana again recalled:

I was living with his older brother and his family and he said 'Well I'm the breadwinner and it's my duty to earn, there's no reason why you should feel pressurised into working and earning money'.

Employment and training - or lack of them - contributed to people's sense of being 'other than' and 'less than' people who more closely approximated the normative view of someone entitled to formal learning or work opportunities. This applied in different ways across all the learner groups.

Employment experiences

Further or higher education generally was lumped together as inappropriate for working class people, for various reasons, and by various 'agents'. Graham, for instance, bemoaned the privileged opportunities of his white collar associates who went to college. These were sometimes the same college courses which could have furthered his own bricklaying career but which he was prevented from attending, without losing a day's pay, because of his work status:

> If you're staff you're paid to go to college because like I mean there's lads working in the town hall and they're doing block release, day release ONC, HNC all this kind of thing.

In spite of the perceived inequity to Graham, it was nevertheless a legitimate common sense power relationship which persisted. White collar workers were simply more entitled (Van Onna 1992). It was a form of naturalised understanding which Bourdieu reserves to explain how higher education sustains its cultural capital in the name of 'habitus'.

Denial and exclusion came in many guises. For Carol it was a case of once you fail you will always be branded a failure. Carol's condition and her ultimately debilitating dismissal experience interlaced with further rationalities as she tried to seek re-employment. Her disability, which had hitherto been unconnected to her mental state, now became synonymous: 'They said well what did they sack you for and I said because you know I'd been ill you know, me condition - that was it'.

A different range of rationales was constructed round Paul's disability, but with the same relentlessness, throughout his life. Although Paul demonstrated considerable ability to find and sustain his own employment, he was consistently treated differently by the employment agency from non

101

disabled people (Barnes 1991). After eight years of work he became unemployed for two years. When most people obtain unemployment benefit because they are seeking work, Paul was obliged to first demonstrate his continued fitness for work - a particular kind of prejudice which Morris (1991) associates with difference. He said: 'I was told I would have to go back to my doctor to get a certificate off him to say that I could still claim unemployment benefit'. What happened next neatly reveals, again, the circulatory nature of power which is located in the network of discourses which produces shared arguments for excluding, rather than including difference:

> My GP then said: 'Well, rather than put you on unemployment benefit we'll put you on invalidity benefit.' So I went to Mitre House for a medical and they wanted to know why I was working in the first place because in their opinion I shouldn't have been.

Paul has not worked since. Yet his condition only worsened after an accident a few years earlier. Like Carol, Paul also accepted certain rationalities in relation to his career ambitions, though one wonders if this argument will always hold true: 'I've always said I'd like to join the police force. But because of my disability I knew I wouldn't qualify'.

The point in identifying these forms of discourse lies in their collective strength to exclude people 'in terms of their deviance from an imagined ideal' (Swain and Cameron 1999: 75), rather than include. This had inevitable effects on people's expectations for themselves and of others (Oliver 1996).

Whilst disability had its own discourses, the Loamshire women had another set of issues to contend with, in addition to any gender discourses from their own culture. Racism came in many guises - as orientalism, as well as more overt discrimination. The Loamshire women would experience orientalism from within and outside their community.

Race issues

Orientalism is a distinctive power mechanism, a form of super cultural capital which divisively re-defines people's perception of what is acceptable behaviour in different contexts (Parmar 1988, Woollett et al 1997). It dominated the Asian women in subtle and often unchallenged ways. Most of the time the women assumed an internalised acceptance that their qualifications, the way they were treated, the type of job entitlement,

102

somehow deserved to be naturally inferior to white people. When other Asian people acquired an identity with the Western culture, however, this created a form of intra-racism which reinforced the new arrival's sense of inferiority.

The most significant example of this kind of orientalism was the way some of the women felt that British born Asian girls reacted to Asian born women. Shivani, for example recalled a British born Asian supermarket cashier who refused to help her with translation difficulties:

I do find that they do look down upon us - and they think because we're from India we're thick and we don't know this and we don't now that ... they see us as a burden, as a problem really and rather than help us, explain to us, they don't do that.

No wonder, then, that so many, as tutor Afsar pointed out, never really wanted to see themselves as British (Bains 1988): 'Because that means you deny your identity, your creed, your religion, your culture' (Afsar). Again Afsar's sentiments bear some resemblance to the working class resistance to university education identified by Karen which will be discussed later in chapters eight and nine.

What was the effect of all these pressures to be excluded? Although the next two chapters will show how individuals fought against their imposed identities, the overwhelming outcome was acceptance - or resignation - to the multiple oppressions. In the end 'disciplinary power' kicked in and no-one had to even convince some of these community learners to stay away from the mainstream of educational provision. Indeed, as the next section shows, the concept of 'selflessness' as a positive, collective purpose, attribute of social capital could be turned in on itself to discourage, rather than encourage educational participation.

Reconstructed rationales for self exclusion

Examples of self surveillance with regard to formal education included a general sense that learning for yourself was somehow 'selfish' (Eric, Julie). Alternatively, they could not be 'clever enough' (Sheila, Peggy, Eric); with a resultant expressed desire only to learn superficially with 'nothing too involved' (Margaret, Emma, Eric, Sheila). Although it was seen as valuable, it was not regarded as a ticket to anywhere beyond what was immediately available.

Having already identified university people as different from themselves, other rationalities such as distance or age, or the ability of ordinary people to cope with university demands (rather than the university's ability to develop the ordinary individual) seemed natural extensions of reasons for non-participation. For example, in line with much literature which criticises stereotypical myths of ageing (Battersby 1984, Hockey & James 1993, Johnston & Phillipson 1983, Baltes & Baltes 1990), age was a consideration which inhibited university study for Muriel: 'Older people learn at a different rate to younger people ... and our grasp of technology isn't quite the same'. Yet Muriel had just taken part in a course which was attended by 30 year olds as well as 70 year olds. Muriel and others did make a distinction between their preferred study and higher levels of learning though. Muriel did not want to avoid education altogether: 'You're never too old to learn'; but put boundaries on her own level of entitlement. The age factor seemed an unconscious self-controlling rationale for abstaining from higher education as distinct from other forms of learning.

The Wyrevale participants felt even further removed from the possibilities of further or higher education - and even work - in terms of class, social experiences and disability backgrounds. Confirming recent literature on the subject (Rieser 1992) Carol, for instance, eventually colluded with those in authority by constructing her own logic to justify and legitimate some of the attitudes to her: 'I suppose really it was getting, that shop job, was getting too much for me really'. As a result of repeated experiences of this nature, the inevitability of Wyrevale then formed its own sequential logic: 'There's nowhere else to go'. By 1993 she had been at Wyrevale eighteen years.

Disability and class-related discourses, when manipulated by those with authority to know and within the rationalities of their time, produced an almost unassailable combination of prejudices through which individuals were expected to find their own empowered voice. Even Gillian, who in many respects challenged normative perceptions that her physical condition meant she was not able, managed to get caught up in various 'desires' to conform when it came to seeking adult education:

> I've always wanted to do it but then again I just thought I was too old you know ... I've always wanted to better myself but I've always just been that wee bit frightened to approach people to see how far my education ... level could take me.

Or if she did get that far: 'I put my name forward for the course in the college and I started wi' a test, right I passed, but no transport'. Three contributory factors appeared to prevent Gillian from pursuing what she most desired - a better education. First it was an assumption that she was too old; then it was lack of confidence; finally it was transport. Whilst Gillian's relatively recent wheelchair acquisition did, indeed, require specialist transport her whole experience and expectation of education was one from which she had been cut off and excluded. It was natural, therefore, to unconsciously want not to do it now.

Paul, a wheelchair user of some four years, had been prevented from accessing some adult education opportunities. But years of interrupted schooling and dependency on medical advice were taking their toll on his will to deviate or 'do wrong' from the expected norm for disabled people. This reply was in response to an invitation to consider education options now: 'I don't know whether I would be able to manage ... in my present situation'; and to a future job: 'I suppose it would depend on what the medical advice would say'. Michael's sense of non-entitlement even extended to what he had already achieved. His string of first aid qualifications were only revealed by accident. He had previously said that he had no qualifications. When asked why the first aid had not been mentioned before he replied: 'I didn't think that would qualify that's why I didn't bother'. The assumption appeared to be that if he, a disabled working class man, had qualifications this must mean that they were of meaningless value, particularly in educational terms. This image would, of course, be reinforced at every turn. He highlighted, for example, how his own knowledge is often only accepted as authority when spoken by a designated expert:

> Then we write to the City Council's Access officer whose job it is to make sure they do that sort of thing and then he goes to the council and says: 'I believe the disabled drivers have been asking for these disabled bays, why haven't you put them in?' And they go and put them in because he's told them to put them in.

The Loamshire women rarely felt they had knowledge from Pakistan or India which had 'authority to know', or which could be privileged over Western knowledges (Said 1995, Avari 1995). Sometimes even the status of being a Pakistani born woman would prevent them from using knowledge which girls with English born status would feel powerful enough to use. This was particularly so in Loamshire X. Sanam, for instance, got remarkably close to Sheila's distinction that intelligence only belonged to people of a different generation from herself:

105

Girls in England are intelligent and confident enough to know what their rights are and they will demand them. They are not afraid whereas girls from Pakistan, girls like me are very afraid to ask for what we are entitled to.

Indeed the combined influence of cultural attitudes to gender and orientalism meant that Sanam now reconstructed her whole view of her place in the world (Brah 1994). She had a sense of being trapped in the assumed inevitability of an unhappy marriage and its perceived regulatory power over her life, exacerbated by her sense of isolation in a foreign country:

It's the system and you're all taken with it and ... I always think about my parents and think what will the repercussions be if I leave him. ... and I also think, well you know if I am not with him, what quality of life will I have? ... I just think I'm dependent on him in the sense that, what would I do if I did not have him, how would I get by, how would I survive? And then, you know I also think if I did leave him, say I went back to Pakistan, how long would my parents be able to look after me ... they are going to die one day and then who on earth looks after me ... so I have to think about all the future and these things and I just feel it is a set pattern of life. You get married and you live with somebody and I suppose that is what I have to do. It just seems pretty natural to stick with him.

With echoes of Lesley's and Mavis' descriptions of people who succumb to disability images of themselves, Sanam's last statement shows just how central disciplinary power can be in suppressing resistance. Sanam was the only participant with a professional career. In her assumed unchangeable existence and confusion Sanam forgot her teaching qualifications and potential for economic self sufficiency if she did return to Pakistan. The cultural discourse of marriage and its connection with honour ('Izzat' - Wilson 1976, Haw 1998) would be difficult to resist for Sanam, in spite of having been the most independent and self sufficient female respondent of all.

All these experiences and their resultant internalisation of ability, rights or opportunities would influence the participants' future ambitions. For some of the Loamshire women, these ambitions were invested in a varied mix of Asian cultural capital and Western orientalism. This mixture directed their ambitions differentially, depending on which combination of discourses were most powerful and what generation they belonged to.

Ambitions amongst the younger generation

The Loamshire women found themselves on a power base of shifting sand. Caught between two cultures, they experienced and re-experienced change which for some meant re-assessment of their familiar relationships with parents, in-laws, husbands, communities and the general public. For some Britain meant loss of personal power, for others it was a gain.

A feature which affected some of the women was the currency in England of their own cultural capital. Significantly this affected the Loamshire Y women differently from those in Loamshire X. Shivani's mother was a teacher, her brother was at a scholarship school in India, her husband and in-laws all had professional jobs in England. Shivani's own ambition was to 'get a nice office job' and have a career. Madhun, similarly, had relatives in commerce and banking and her in-law family were well established professionals in England, with ambitions that Madhun should follow suit.

The discourse of the West, however, would affect how those ambitions could be achieved. The Loamshire Y women knew that if they were to maintain their status in this country, cultural capital included more than qualifications. They had two obstacles to overcome. Firstly an understanding that ethnocentrism already devalued their academic achievements (Joseph et al 1990). As Shivani said: 'If I had a degree and all that from India here they would only value my education up to the O level standard'; or in Cohen's (1988) words: 'Whenever black people threatened to ... enter history on their own terms a further strategy of misrepresentation was mobilised' (p. 20). As with Portside and Wyrevale, these discourses would have their disciplinary power effect on the women. Their perception, for instance, of the gap they had to bridge as Indian, rather than English educated people, included a need to speak English like the English:

Our pronunciation and everything is so different ... this is why we need such courses so we can ... become more compatible to them [the English] (Madhun);

... I've learned that when we write notes to our teachers we must always address as Dear Mr or Mrs instead of writing dear teacher and not to forget to write thank yous and please, because sometimes we come across, the way we say things, as a bit rude, you know (Shila).

The desire to acquire appropriate mannerisms suggests that for the Indian middle class women, at least, they had already internalised a social racism which meant they needed more than acquisition of knowledge - it also meant acquiring the internalised code of that culture: 'Racism promotes whiteness as the norm' (Aziz, 1997: 72).

The social environment in which the younger Loamshire Y women were placed indicated a different set of values from the Loamshire X women. Shivani had left India just before completing her A level equivalents. She said:

> In India I was educated and I was asked if I wanted to keep on learning and I'm here and there's all these opportunities and I don't want to stop now. I want to carry on and I want to take advantage of that ... I want to learn more English ... do more technology and filing.

Disciplinary power now included a desire for education, training and a place in the skilled job market (Bhachu 1991). English was no longer just a means to 'get by', but an essential requirement for a good job. As has already been mentioned, however, the assumptions that English language skills and further training would supersede the women's own high qualifications from India were barely questioned (Mukherjee 1988). Shila for example, with A levels from India, lowered her Indian goals of a good administration job, but still set her sights on a place in the local economy beyond her current factory or cleaning experiences. Shila's original goals in India were to complete her degree course and teach like her mother; but now:

> I would like to improve my English further and get a better job. When I say better job I mean I know I'm not very capable of very high profile jobs because you know educated people are struggling to get good jobs but I will be quite happy to get a job in a store as a cashier on a till (Shila).

For people like Shila, Madhun, Shivani and Sabia, learning English was also a normalising strategy for social inclusion. It acted as a form of control over how the women were allowed to function economically. The argument which the women absorbed was that learning English was an essential [but most difficult to overcome] passport to the job market, irrespective of their existing skills: 'Because everywhere you go you need English now, especially if you want to get a job, then you need to have English skills' (Sabia). 'Common sense' rationalities always dismissed the idea that bilingual or mother tongue (as opposed to English only) study might result in higher skills achievement for the women, and that some jobs at least could be performed equally well through Punjabi or other languages (Milburn 1996).

108

In contrast, ambitions amongst the Wyrevale and Portside groups were influenced by two things. Firstly they had few qualifications on which to draw; secondly they had lived through a longer period of adulthood which reinforced their present position. So none of the Wyrevale group expected to work again, irrespective of their employability age ('I know I'll never work again' - Dave, age 48). The Portside group, too, were happy to stay within the local expectations of their town. Although the next chapters show that their community learning achievements were beginning to influence their sense of what they were capable of, the ceiling that they set on their educational ambitions was reinforced by long-standing images of higher education and who was entitled to a university education.

Who goes to university?

> There is this ivory tower, there is this image of this mad professor who will speak god knows what and you won't understand a word he's saying and he will have this funny suit and a waistcoat and tweak tie (Karen).

Maintenance of the status quo was articulated in three ways. Firstly a lingering perception, identified by Jackson and Marsden as far back as 1973, that universities were out of this world and therefore out of reach for local people. Margaret, for instance spoke for many when she said: 'Well, [they'd think] it'd be a foreign country and never aspire to go there .. it's way above them'. The reproductive and divisive element of cultural capital started with the grammar school - both as a symbol of advantage to employers: 'People would think you ... were better educated or ... be able to adapt to the job better' (Margaret) and also as a signifier of difference at school: 'It seemed as though the better type of children obviously were going to go to the grammar school' (Eric). Sheila, whose father was a teacher but who herself went to a secondary modern, made an insightful linguistic observation which highlights cultural capital's particularly naturalised discourse from 'the rest': 'They talk differently don't they, people that are intelligent ... they skim over a lot of things, whereas I need to fit the bits to fill in' (age 40). Sheila was talking about 'university people'. Like its culture, university intelligence is associated with a different linguistic code - in this case one which misses out certain link words or concepts. Intelligence in relation to universities becomes a reified and inborn culture which excludes, rather than includes other intelligences born from different stock.

Perhaps unsurprisingly there were only two kinds of personal observations regarding higher education. On the one hand: 'I never really thought about it' (Margaret, Peggy, Eric, Emma); on the other hand if it was briefly contemplated it was then dismissed as 'above my head' (Emma, Peggy, Sheila). Graham simply stated that you were not expected to go to university if you were from 'round here'.

Disciplinary power therefore was complex and built on the effect of previous discourses and experiences. Their combined outcome could be to reinforce 'otherness' and a contradictory, unconscious 'desire' to be excluded in spite of the apparent desire for a sense of inclusiveness. The process, of course, would silence participation in the wider world and discourage the very acts of self direction now expected of adult learners.

This chapter has demonstrated just some of the regulatory power mechanisms which the learners had to overcome. The emphasis in describing these examples is not to show how helpless the world of difference is, but to demonstrate how few people are aware of the strength of dominant power relations in producing certain kinds of behaviour. The next chapter will provide examples where some of the participants contested these consistent messages from schools, the medical world and employers of their denied right to access, to decisions, economic autonomy and educational opportunities.

8 Combating social exclusion: being inclusive about difference

Introduction

> We have to argue that those experiencing social exclusion have a voice but we need also to be able to conceptualise that voice (Williams 1998: 25).

One aim of this study is to conceptualise the cultural, structural and social power relations which surround and silence the marginalised voice. The life experiences of people could mean that they contributed to their own silences and social exclusion. This book also argues that university adult education excludes by not recognising those different voices. The experience of difference also gave people a different way of seeing the world. In some cases this meant they had access to knowledge which was 'privileged' to their connection with disability, class, culture or gender. As a result individuals would reveal critical and analytical thinking on subject matter which is often ignored by those with authority to know. Educational inclusion means that we must recognise those different ways of knowing and doing within our mainstream learning programmes. The community programme offered some examples of how this was possible.

It must be remembered that hardly any of the community learners had participated in formal provision for several years. None had taken part in university courses, very few had any school qualifications and many were not considered capable, as children, of learning at a higher level. Some of their stories of how they learned are therefore quite remarkable. Specific examples of organised learning initiatives came from John, the steelmaker, now seventy years old, Graham the bricklayer in his thirties, sixty two year old Peggy who started her working life in a factory, mother of three Kajal who also started out as a factory worker and Gillian who attended special school and was now in her mid forties. There were other examples of insight and understanding worthy of higher learning levels. Some people, who were less confident about describing specific learning initiatives, demonstrated critical understanding of everyday issues based on their own life experiences. The community courses allowed them to capitalise on these more differentiated values.

This chapter then, serves three purposes. Firstly, to show what kind of learning the participants had undertaken by themselves, in spite of expectations. Secondly I want to show how they used knowledge on their terms. The need to identify different ways of knowing for black women has been argued by Hill Collins (1990). I would argue that this principle can also apply to other minority groups as well. In these examples it is depth of understanding which we are looking for, rather than conventional wisdom about appropriate learning. The third section gives the participants an opportunity to identify what was important about the community courses. These latter comments contrast with liberal academic perceptions about what is important for university courses. The examples also reinforce Williams' argument that the socially excluded should be seen as actors in their own right rather than simply normalised into the dominant model of learning behaviour (1998: 9).

Learning which was important for me - challenging 'normality'

It was not considered normal for working class people to study anything on an intellectual level - as earlier chapters have shown. Anyone who attempted to do so was pretty much out on a limb. They would be unsupported compared with their middle class counterparts. Indeed, many in this book experienced active discouragement of such an interest. Furthermore, their focus of interest would not necessarily fit the abstract subject areas in higher education institutions. Learning therefore manifested itself in different ways.

In many ways Chris did study a conventional topic, but in a very specific context. Chris, confident in his working class status and culture, spoke with pride about a steelmaking job which he loved and which was part of his family heritage. He described his childhood role of delivering his father's sandwiches on double shift days:

> On my way, my journey through the works, the iron works and the steel works, I went through the steel making section and I became ... very interested in the way those men, what those men were doing. And I was fascinated by what they did and I realised then that that would probably be what I wanted to do.

Chris concluded his story of his induction into steel making with commitment and authority: 'I found it very satisfying to make ... good steel

... it was a good feeling ... you felt as though you'd done a good job'. Yet steel making had neither authoritative power nor status. Even in the working class hierarchy, whilst being skilled work it was not classed as a trade. It proved, however, both empowering to Chris and an unrecognised link with academic study. When the opportunity to train for electric steel making arrived Chris volunteered. He described how he capitalised on this opportunity through private reading and talking to more experienced colleagues:

> I got as many books out as I could of the library in different places and did what I could on me own to er improve my own education on the chemistry side of it ... so that when I did go away ... I was talking to people who were in a similar situation ... I was able to understand what they were telling me ... so really it was a question of reading quite a lot and trying to understand it and of course talking to other people as well.

This independent learning process follows an almost classic example of the traditional practice of academic learning identified in chapter five - a combination of text books, reading and seminars or tutorials. Although this was a vocationally linked initiative, it was Chris's personal interest in metallurgy which drove him to study beyond what was required for the job. Indeed he said if there had been a local opportunity to study metallurgy, one which also accommodated his shift work, he would have taken it. This is one of several individual stories across the Portside interviews which revealed unsupported attempts at further study in a climate which claimed that education was not necessary for, or desired by, working class people. There is evidence, however, from research relating to the 1980s that:

> Although relatively few adults recorded themselves as participants in adult education in the formal sense, many were actively engaged in organised learning projects (Schuller & Bostyn 1993: 367).

The paradox here is that learning is now being promoted in public debate as if it hadn't been desired before. Of course, if you provide courses which take no account of working class job patterns (such as shift work) then incentives to study will fade. There is now an assumed present day change of interest by the working class population in learning because systems are becoming more flexible. However, the notion that all working class interests lie in vocational learning, as evidenced by the promotion of NVQs, does not match the trend of the following examples. The question must be asked then - are the providers dictating what people are interested in, or is

113

the system really being market led? Higher education for most of the community learners was valued more for its personal development qualities than work-related goals.

Not all the participants wanted to cultivate knowledge associated with their surroundings. Where Chris exploited his environment and culture as a resource for study, Peggy fought against the attitudes of her generation towards girls and schooling. Her tenuous association with a thwarted grammar school place gave her a different vision for herself. She obtained two O levels by correspondence course as a teenager. During the year her father died, she negotiated with a local school to let her sit the exams alongside its school pupils. She studied while working long hours in a factory:

> I found it very difficult because I was working in a factory, trying to study at home and I was just too tired, you know ... you could only do like really once a fortnight if you will because I worked shift work so when you were on morning shift you had the afternoon to work but you were kind of tired after you'd been up at six o'clock in the morning ... it tended to be hard work really and when you were on afternoon shift of course you didn't finish till ten o'clock so you really hadn't much chance at all.

The isolated efforts of this young woman who was also orphaned during the same period can only be admired. Resistance against normality therefore took many forms. For some it was the voice of individuals trying to break through the social climate of their time and the arguments associated with both class and gender which assumed the predictability of their lives. In the face of the range of discourses already outlined in chapters six and seven, this was a brave and, at time, almost impossible task.

Tutor Kajal, from a working class Indian family, but educated in England, was prepared to take risks that no one else amongst the Muslim and Pakistani women did. She challenged the ideology of her caste, contested the identity placed on her by her family and employers and gave her own authority to an inner belief that she could be part of cultural capital's professional classes. Where others failed or had given up, Kajal continued at considerable personal cost (see also Ali 1992). She described her determination to achieve a teaching degree against her family's wishes:

> I told him [access tutor]: 'I don't want to stop here Eric. I want to do something, I want to work with young children.' ... I stayed up late at night, you know, like 2 0' clock in the morning to do my work. But I was really, I was doing it for myself and I wanted to prove I could do it ... I pushed myself, I said: 'No I can't

114

stop here;' and I did my TP [teaching practice] third year TP while I was seven months pregnant as well.

Sometimes resistances against expected lifestyles were not specifically course related. Nevertheless several examples demonstrated how hard it was to get your voice heard - to be perceived as capable. Gillian and Paul with cerebral palsy and attending special schools had to fight against images of their ability to do anything, let alone pursue a career or further study. Both shared similar characteristics of tenacity against persistent attempts to 'normalise' them with negative identities throughout their lives. Gillian cited one instance in her early teens. She wanted a two wheeler bike like the one belonging to her next door cousin. Her parents would only contemplate a three wheeler: 'I said I'm no having a three wheeler - not at my age, I'm no babe - a three wheeler bike - no way'. She persuaded her cousin to let her practice:

> So I set out to prove to them that I could ride this wee bike ... I kept falling off it and then I got that I could kind of ride it ... and then I learned to go round and round ... and that's how I got ma bike ... it was great, it was really good.

Gillian's continued resistance to other people's construction of her disabled identity meant she would re-position herself as a member of society and 'normalise' herself on her own terms. Where marriage and motherhood for most women have been articulated as a form of oppression by feminist writers, for disabled people such status could mean an increased sense of self because automatic right of access to such everyday experiences was often denied (Morris, 1991, Lonsdale 1990). Gillian worked, married and had two sons in the same social world as her peers and siblings.

These stories demonstrate how much tenacity and effort went into even small achievements. Little wonder then, that few people saw their way beyond what doctors, teachers, family and community had already decided for them.

Outright resistance to their own cultural expectations was rare amongst the Loamshire women who were educated abroad - though, as the earlier chapters have already shown, - some were better educated than this book's generation of Western participants. Nevertheless, whilst Hinaa was not prepared to challenge the practices of her immediate community's fears that higher education might lead girls astray, she did openly disagree with the principle:

I go against most people's ideas, my opinion is that ... if you're going to go along the wrong tracks then you will do right from school, you don't need to leave home to do that ... I don't think too much education is a bad thing and I don't think universities affect your thought or corrupt you.

The notion that universities do not 'affect your thought' is an interesting concept in view of earlier discussions about the meaning of 'higher' education. Unfortunately there is not space to explore this here. Women from all the social groups showed, however, that open resistance to normative expectations can have a high price.

Another form of resistance could be seen with Margaret from Portside and Sanam from Loamshire. Both women transferred their personal ambitions onto their children. This is a form of vicarious existence which many working class mothers adopted as a means of contesting the identity bestowed on themselves by their immediate generation (West 1997, Jackson & Marsden 1973). For Sanam the issues were more complexly tied up with cross-nation, intergenerational and cultural issues. But the outcome was the same:

I've changed in my ambitions for me. I am more interested in my son's education now. I want him to study and I want him to get a good job ... I want him to be able to stand on his own two feet. And that's how I bring him up.

There were other ways in which people's differences manifested themselves from standardised expectations of learners. These were nearly always to do with culturally and socially specific types of knowledge or learning. The next section looks at how some very much wanted to acquire knowledge on their terms.

Learning which is important for me - my way of seeing the world

Some people challenged mainstream providers' images of what and how they were expected to learn. Karen and Eric, for instance, both questioned the middle class nature of teachers, particularly at university level. Even as a child Eric was caught up with a working class discourse that tried to 'de-capitalise' the culture of grammar school children: 'They would be called weird ones that went to grammar school'. Even today he associated middle class tutors with a self assumed superiority:

116

I wouldn't want one that talked down to you ... some people who are far better off than you ... who talk rather posh ... that's the only kind of tutor I wouldn't like to have.

Similarly, liaison worker Karen, often speaking on behalf of her peers, questioned the dominant educational ideology that the only worthwhile form of progress and progression was one which required an upward spiral of achievements: 'There isn't to go so far is an achievement - it's to go so far and no further is classed as a failure'. She insisted therefore that courses should be provided in Portside with one proviso: 'What they did with that knowledge was up to them'. Karen ultimately made her own judgement about whether the cultural shift required by a formal educational ethos was worth the effect of losing her own working class identity and sense of self:

Do they get to the point where they say do I become one of them or do I say no, your ways are not always right and they ... have to make that decision and then it comes back again to do I want it enough?

The colonisation of social class in education is an issue which Lynch and O'Neill (1994) claim is a central inequality experienced by working class people:

If they are to succeed in the education system they have to abandon certain features of their class background. They cease to be working class at least to some degree. Other oppressed or marginalised groups in education do not lose their defining minority identity or status by being educated (p.307).

The exclusiveness of this experience might be contested by other minority groups (Bird, 1996 for example), but the concern that the middle classes colonise formal education has a long legacy (Simon 1990, Lynch & O'Riordan 1998). So, if they rejected the dominant and prescribed models for valuable knowledge, what did people replace it with? And how were they demonstrating equal, but different kinds of higher learning?

Graham and Tony referred to specific learning initiatives. Several Portside women, the Loamshire women and Michael from Wyrevale showed how they were able to use their own privileged way of seeing the world to enhance learning and knowledge in a broader sense. Graham's description is the most remarkable since it directly contradicts LA1's critique of family history in chapters three and four. Graham first of all explained how he continued with his family history studies by negotiating with his wife (who did not attend the course) to do some of the research while he was at work:

> G: You make time ... nip into town and half an hour in the library ... M_____ does a lot of reading
> M: I do a lot of the research, Graham then looks at it and then he tells me what pointers to look for the next time.

Their learning progress followed the very goals and critical, questioning approach advocated by the liberal education academics - but through a topic which LA1 regarded as not acceptable for higher level study. Graham and his wife enthusiastically discussed how they used oral history and official records to build up their own picture of social conditions through time:

> You come across a lot of sort of local history, sort of social history as you're looking through like the formation of the town ... certain streets ... cause we go up to it and say: 'It won't be there, because that wasn't built yet. Well, do I know that?' Like the back of Hartington Street; there wasn't anything there in 1881. We know that just by looking through ... newspaper cuttings ... I mean just noticing the difference ... in the way they report an incident between like 1900 and today ... the way they wrote the reports, the court case ... they're colourful ... the writing ... we're talking to family members and they start telling you stories that you never heard of ... so you're looking in old newspapers to try and find a report of this particular thing ... We're now encouraging people to tell stories which were never written down.

These remarks combine systematic enquiry, text appreciation, comparison and contrast, discovery of new evidence; all proclaimed essential qualities for higher education learning (Barnett 1990, McNair 1997). Their goal, however, was not further academic study - but the development of a private library of evidence in their own house and a recorded legacy for future generations. The wider community goal for the family history students as a whole was to form a family history society. Now, several years on, this society has a thriving membership of over 200 names. The relationship between this kind of activity and the notion of social capital as an indicator of social arrangements which: 'promote communication, reflexivity and mutual learning' (Schuller & Burns 1999: 54) has already been referred to. The significance for Portside was that the learning was on their terms.

Tony, from Wyrevale, was more isolated in his efforts. He had literacy difficulties and bitter memories of school where: 'There wasn't a teacher who wanted to teach yer'. He had an artificial leg and developed an interest in prosthetics:

I got some different books in the libraries ... I got clocking them out - about four books I went through and I've wrote about a thousand page ... and transferred onto a disc onto a printout, but that's only as far as er limbs are concerned ... I've not gone as far as er hearing aids, glasses, teeth, what have you, which I want to do.

Tony's level of understanding for academic inquiry was less sophisticated than Graham's but then so was his education. He was fifteen years older than Graham and, as a labourer with a leg amputation, had already been unemployed for more than eight years. Again the key points here are not Tony's use of literacy skills but the topic he chose to study and his own willingness to develop his inquiry within a broader context, but relevant to his immediate experiences.

A number of women were less confident about identifying individual learning projects. They drew on their experiential knowledge for different purposes. The women's accumulated personal knowledge, for instance, often derived from experiences of other people's suffering, or caring for other people (Gladys, Sheila, Muriel, Julie, Margaret), and of personal deprivation (Peggy, Gladys, Margaret). Some of these experiences helped them analyse the present. Peggy described how she would intuitively assess medical needs in her job as medical secretary. (This is probably a strategy which doctors are trained to use all the time):

I don't ask questions, just observances. I sort of judge people, some people you can joke with, other people you can never get away with it ... I mean you're not conscious of doing it or anything ... like the telephone, you can tell where people are feigning an illness to get an appointment, things like that (Peggy).

Understanding of human relations in the present also translated into a more critical awareness of other people's needs, responsibilities and personal growth:

I think children bring you out a lot. You meet people and you have got to teach them to go out into the world and grow up. You have to prove to them that you can do things (Sheila).

For the women their perceived role was primarily a class and gender specific one of carer - but a role which they appropriated to provide a rich source of reflection in practice (reflexivity). Muriel, for example, described how she extended this role into work:

119

When I worked I was assistant manageress but I was I suppose to some degree I was everybody's agony aunt because if anybody had a problem they always came to me and I always spared the time to try and help them at least to listen to them (Muriel).

Muriel had cared for both in-laws and now her ninety one year old mother. She, Sheila and Chris all gave examples of how emotion and reason together form and build rational arguments from local circumstances. They would critique their experience of emotions. In the process they produced knowledge which could be transferable, with or without supporting text material. Muriel used her acquired caring skills, for example, to help others critically appraise their own situations, with an almost textbook application of humanistic counselling theory:

Sometimes you don't have to do anything physically, you don't even have to say a word to help somebody, you just have to listen. And, as they talk, very often they sort out their own problem because just talking to somebody who's prepared to sit there and listen to them, they can see themselves where they're going wrong or which avenue they should be taking.

The focus on analysing family and people was also transferable to the study of family history and extends the social capital concept of which societal arrangements stimulate reflexivity.

Emotion was not the only source of additional knowledge. Sara drew on her experience of Pakistan's formal, rote learning approaches to teaching, to make analytical judgements about the teaching on her welfare rights course:

I realised there are different methods of learning especially because you emphasised general points rather than specific details, although we had all the details in the booklets. Obviously there are important legal points which you emphasised but there again they were just general points and it wasn't a question of writing them down it was more a question of listening to you and talking.

It is unlikely that a class of teenage undergraduates would be able to critique their own educational experiences any better than this.

Feminist literature on 'ways of knowing' and 'experience' has developed over the years. Gilligan (1979) and Westcott (1979) for instance, claimed distinctive characteristics for women's approach to knowledge on these lines, which Belenky et al (1986) identified as 'subjective knowledge': 'a perspective from which truth and knowledge are conceived of as personal, private and subjectively known or intuited' (p.15). Code (1991) criticises Belenky et al's position because they then described subjective knowledge as a phase of development on the way to more male-associated 'constructed knowledge', thereby reinforcing the already existing and hierarchical distinction between experience and knowledge: 'such that accumulated experience neither counts as knowledge nor is regarded as its source' (p.241). Skeggs (1997) develops Code's argument by claiming that experience needs to be tested in order to gain official knowledge status. Nevertheless it should also be seen - like all knowledge - as not fixed: 'in either time or place' (p.27).

However, in order for any knowledge to acquire status the knowledge and its knower have to be recognised in the first place. For most of these learners their knowledge was, in Foucault's terms, 'subjugated and 'delegitimated'. In other words, anyone with any status or ability to influence, simply did not recognise that such knowledge was important or relevant. Amita, one of the Loamshire tutors identified a way in which the dominant Western world did recognise her own culturally specific knowledge. It was done as a form of exploitation, however, rather than as a recognition of her equal authority to know (Said 1995, Shaheed 1994, Mohanty 1990). Amita explained how she was expected to extend her low-paid, low status, 'link worker' role of translator between Asian women patients and the health service:

> I was training staff, student nurses on aspects of the Asian culture and that started about ten years ago. I actually facilitated a few courses but that wasn't appreciated. I ran a course for the tutors there as well and you know, I mean you do a lot because your title is link worker, but that's all - you can't progress from there.

Amita was not the only one to have her subjugated knowledge exploited in this way. Paul was disabled and working class. He too had knowledge that was privileged to his experiences as a disabled person. He amply demonstrated how he could use that knowledge as a learning tool for those in authority. He also could transfer that understanding to speak on behalf of other, differentiated and often excluded groups. Nevertheless, his contribution was only accepted in a voluntary capacity through committees. He cited an example of how the Disabled Drivers Association would encourage the City Council to review its pavement layout:

> We advise the local authority to do something and do it a specific way so that it helps not just wheelchair users. If we, say they put a drop kerb for instance, it's not just helping a wheelchair user to get across a road, it's helping a blind person with a stick because they know if they go to a drop kerb it's flat and level and

they don't have to trip over a kerb to get across the road. It helps young mums with pushchairs, because they don't have to bounce the push chair off the pavement on the one side and then bounce it back onto the other side.

The issue here is not that Paul, as a wheelchair user, knows what his wheelchair can do (though he obviously did have that knowledge as well), but it raises the issue of marginality, inclusiveness and representation. By giving status to knowledge which is based on the experiences of particular social groups, this raises the possibility for new dialogues and the use, rather than abuse, of power between differences. In the same way that the local environment changes once disabled people are taken into account, so do the curriculum and teaching methods in a classroom.

The community courses were not all perfect examples of teaching and learning. They attempted, however, to make previously subjugated knowledges visible and give credence to their knowers. Both tutors and participants described how the courses enabled this to happen.

Learning which has been important for me - the community courses

Karen's influence over the Portside learning milieu continued with her choice of venue, tutor and subject. The participants' subsequent comments highlighted three interconnecting factors: 'Well, it just seemed like a relaxed atmosphere, it was easier to take things in, there didn't seem to be any pressure on you at all' (Graham). The atmosphere and lack of pressure were key themes for many of the learners. These are taken up by many writers on behalf of older learners (Shea 1990, Withnal & Percy 1994, Harrison 1993), though their applicability clearly stretches beyond age specificity. Another theme was the communal, sharing nature of the learning environment:

It was sort of a common interest - everybody was sort of interested in .. everybody else's ... family history. You know, ... if they'd done any themselves ... where they'd been, how they'd acquired any information (Graham).

The third feature was the tutor's own willingness to share his personal experiences as teaching material:

I: Give an example of how he made it interesting
A: Well, by relating about his own family history ... what he'd found out and how he'd found it and what surprises he'd had (Julie).

122

These comments resemble the teacher-learner relationship outlined by CA1 and CA4 amongst the community academic staff. The learning environment relied on a shared experiential knowledge base of, to different degrees, mutual learning. This again is a style advocated by promoters of learning for older adults, often described as 'gerogogy' (Battersby 1990: 133). In gerogogy education is a collective enterprise and a process which: 'will leave [learners] in control of their own thinking rather than in the control of the thinking of others' (Battersby 1984: 78). The aspect of mutuality even revealed itself in who enrolled. Seventy percent of the Portside participants enrolled with a family member or friend. Their comradeship continued throughout the course. Indeed Karen reinforced Graham's point by highlighting the interactive behaviour of the group as a whole:

> And I found it brilliant how the people who knew so much worked well with the people who were real beginners and one wasn't trying to overshadow the other at all.

The issue of mutuality, of course, is a critical feature of social capital. It also came up in the other groups. Lesley, a tutor for Wyrevale pointed out that the participants 'differences' could be normalised in their own reciprocal atmosphere of acceptance:

> Whatever happens, people understand. If somebody has a fit or is unable to do something that most normal people could do or somebody eats in a peculiar way or, you know, does bizarre things then in a group of people who understand then you feel safe. One of the rules is that it doesn't matter if you walk differently ... the other rule is ... you don't probe into someone else's disability, you accept it ... so there is an acceptance there which there isn't in the outside world.

Tony confirmed the value of trust as a feature of the learning atmosphere:

> We haven't been rushed; ... it was very informal; ... we were learning in little groups; ... it was to the persons and feedback; ... we helped each other and talked in little groups (Tony).

In terms of this overall learning approach Paul echoed Tony and Karen's comments. The important factors were learning pace and a shared learning relationship:

> Well we haven't been rushed with the course that's one thing and as regards the paperwork there hasn't been as much paperwork as some ... courses I've had.

123

And er I think er the people we've had in to help with the courses, seem to take more time over how they present the course and give us more time to take it in rather than rush through it like there was in mainstream courses, I think. That's my opinion anyway (Paul).

Until PhD study status is reached, it is significant how much 'learning pace' is a strategy of differentiation. The discourse around 'ability' is often linked to fixed timetables for learning. It is a subtle but powerful way of disabling people's potential if their socio-economic, emotional or practical circumstances require a different timescale (rather than standard, or level) of learning. Perhaps significantly, Halpern (1998) suggests that such features of mutuality and grass roots approaches to learning have much wider potential in addressing social exclusion:

The creation of trust and confidence is as important as the acquiring of information and answers, as is the building of social capital so that the excluded can shape their own solutions rather than have them delivered from above (p.278).

These considerations of course do not sit easily with an education system predicated on individualism and competition. Indeed neither Wyrevale (as a social group) nor Portside (as a family history study cohort) seemed to be building much in the way of investment for acceptance within the mainstream learning society. Their own mutuality did produce localised investments, however, as future sections indicate.

Another aspect of inclusive teaching was the degree to which learners were enabled to share and gain knowledge that was relevant to their interests. Tony showed how synthesis of ideas could emerge from this learning style. Although this interaction used no text, the process he described bore some similarity to academic discussion groups:

At the church it went on different groups and different workshops and different people had different ideas and when you got four or five different ideas put in front of you you thought well that was my idea on the shop we had, but those ideas were also for development ... the good way of learning was [when] different [groups] had different ideas and they all come together and they spoke their own different ways. They amalgamated between each other ... whereas the ones in the college, people picked out of a book or manual which chapter they wanted and ... you knew nothing about this chapter ... so you didn't have a clue.

Tony described a process of exploring different view points, reflection and synthesis. His learning experience combined the essential elements of

124

learning so valued by HOD4 in the academic interviews. But for Tony, text books stifled creativity and development. Textbooks were part of a school system where: 'There wasn't a teacher who wanted to teach yer' and certainly it seems no-one who wanted to teach Tony.

The community tutors struggled hard to disentangle the above mixture of cultural and religious values by providing a curriculum and teaching style which enabled participants to claim their own authority for their subjugated knowledge on their terms (Tisdall & Perry 1997, Preece & Bokhari 1996, Preece 1999a, Dadzie 1993, hooks 1994). This approach relates to the gerogogy articulated by Battersby (1990) earlier in this section and Skeggs' (1997) position on experiential knowledge. Curriculum content, however, was a key to the acceptability of any learning activity. This applied to all three groups and is critical to disability literature (Oliver 1993, Barnes 1991). The discussion here is taken from the Loamshire women. Sara asked of Western provision generally:

> I think they should especially try to understand our religion and offer us courses on our religion rather than things on their communities and on their own way of life … we should not be forced to study their religion for example, you know we have our own, and they ought to realise that. They ought to study about our religion for their own benefit as well, to try and understand us … to find out how we organise our community and how we actually live, sort of on a day to day basis.

Sanam highlighted this issue by citing a number of curricular interests which she studied in Pakistan but which are simply not available in the UK (Said 1995): 'And you can also study in Pakistan history; you can study Iqbal studies, which are about the poet Iqbal, the philosopher'. The absence of learning opportunities with which the women could identify only serves to highlight the sense of difference and otherness which many women felt in a world which made no connection with their lifestyle or beliefs (Buijs 1993).

The CP tutors and participants gave examples of a teaching approach which respected their subjugated knowledges at an experiential, practical and cultural level. Tutor Afsar made a point of drawing on subjugated knowledge:

> I have to make a conscious effort of applying it to the Asian family … otherwise they are not going to see the relevance of it … I try to involve them into a discussion first … and they do start to come out with ideas, now this is because I'm drawing on their experience, so I don't like actually sitting there feeding them information, I try and get the information to come from them;

125

and this was confirmed by participant Shila as a source of critical analysis:

> I remember talking about my experiences, our experiences back in India ... we got to know about each other's knowledge and education back there and we were able to compare this here in this country.

Hooks (1994) describes this process as 'engaged pedagogy':

> Using pedagogical strategies that affirm their presence, their right to speak (p. 84); where ... experience can illuminate and enhance our understanding of academic material (p. 21).

Tisdall and Perry (1997) warn, however, that in a mixed class such an approach must ensure that the dominant voice of, for example, white majorities does not re-silence the minority voice. All the community courses were designed around the needs of minority groups as majority participants for each class. As with the Wyrevale group and many courses in Portside, the teaching relationship was about reducing the power differential between teacher and learner and about recognising subjugated knowledge in the learning environment. In comparison with academic teaching methods, for example, this would entail a different focus. Where the academic staff might use experience as a means of drawing people closer to the text, here the experience was a means of building new knowledge which would inform the text (though Skeggs, 1997 points out that experience, too, must be interrogated). These courses and their style of operating did not challenge the main institution's forms of provision, but did make people insiders on their own courses. On the Loamshire courses, for instance, white women would and could join them if they wanted, but it was on the Asian women's terms.

The Loamshire women particularly valued the bilingual and role model teaching on their courses - a feature supported by Flowers & Sheared (1997), Sherman-Swing (1989) and Majid (1985). Sara's comment was typical:

> You were here as a bilingual tutor and that helped and secondly because you're female and that for me is important and I think it is important for a lot of other Asian women because I have never once held back and had it been a man teaching me I would have held back ... you need a teacher you can approach because then Islamic concepts of who you can see and you can talk to or who you can't talk to, these all come into play and they were overcome.

126

Moreover, in line with those from Portside and Wyrevale, they also commented on a learning environment which was friendly and encouraging:

> The thing that made me more comfortable was the fact that the course was held in the place of worship, the Mandir, the temple, very friendly environment, I felt at ease going there. It wasn't as frightening as walking into a college campus or whatever. (Shila).

To understand their significance, these replies need to be compared with the academic interview descriptions of a good teacher - where the teacher needed to be 'academically our sort', possess a PhD, be up to date with his knowledge field and then, perhaps, have an understanding of the mechanics of teaching (chapter four). Student-teacher relationships were rarely mentioned in academia other than by the community staff.

Whilst environmental features are now commonly understood as desirable motivators for Asian mothers and parents in general (McGivney 1990, Dadzie 1993), the consistency of their replies and their added emphasis on cultural relevance is worth repeating in the total context of the women's responses. It demonstrates how different the adult education world must seem without these re-assuring practices and highlights again that progression courses which simply take place in 'normalised' college environments have the effect of silencing and ignoring these clear messages, even though some might venture into college at a later date. Indeed, although these courses were for non British born women, the community project continues to provide local, culturally specific, courses with bilingual support for an increasing mix of British born and Indian Sub continent women who attend courses together.

This chapter has privileged 'difference'. It has shown the potential of building on the internal social capital of excluded groups. People's ability and motivation to learn can be enhanced by the right environment and social mix of participants, staff and curriculum. There are, however, practical and ethical issues around a learning programme which simply creates other forms of exclusion by separating people out. Chapter eleven will deal with this concern more fully. Nevertheless, there is a message for mainstream providers here. The message is that mainstream continuing education does not provide an obvious bridge to community values. What is appreciated on community courses is simply ignored within the mainstream. People who have already experienced marginalisation for so long, however, also have a fragile sense of self which needs nurturing and recognising far beyond what might otherwise be regarded as simply a first stage return to education in readiness for the mainstream. The process of social inclusion is not a quick fix and chapter nine explores the fragmentation of learner identities, particularly in these crucial transition stages.

9   Changing identities

Each of us lives with a variety of potentially contradicting identities which battle within us for allegiance (Weeks 1990: 58).

Up till now I have talked about the power of discourse (internalised cultural or social values and behaviours) to influence individual decision making and people's sense of entitlement to education. Central to the participants' sense of entitlement, however, was their sense of who they were in relation to other people. A deeper understanding of how people build up such a picture of themselves will help educators provide effective learning programmes for those most excluded from the mainstream.

In chapter two I explained how identities are formed as a result of exposure to different discourses. I introduced the notion of 'subjectivity' - the term used to describe people's personal construction of their conscious and unconscious selves as a way of understanding their relationship with the world. Self image and identity are aspects of people's subjectivities. Subjectivities encompass the way people see themselves in terms of power relationships with others - influenced by, for example, gender, occupation or social status. As such they are subject to new influences which may or may not reinforce old images of the self. This notion of subjectivity has attracted attention from a wide range of writers.

Code (1995) and others emphasise the fluidity of subjectivities. They can encompass multiple identities which are not fixed in time, and which depend on a wide range of variables and social experiences:

Class, race, ethnicity, sexual orientation, economics, religion, age, sexuality, bodily size, ability and other privilegings and marginalisings too numerous to mention produce subjectivities variously throughout their biographical life-lines (p.176).

Educational institutions and other agencies, such as the family, all have a bearing on the evolution of individual subjectivities. Mac an Ghaill, for instance, uses this feminist framework to explain how masculinities are formed:

Students relations with their families were identified as critical in the cultural production of masculinities ... the institutional categorisation of 'academic' and

129

'non academic' routes were crucial elements in the cultural production of different masculinities (p.52).

Skeggs (1994) explains how people then police their own identities in response to the curriculum which in turn shapes their perceived life roles: 'Women would willingly take up subject positions which defend them as responsible caring women with occupational potential' (p.85). Code (1991) reminds us however, that whilst each individual's location in time and space is a construction brought about by power relations, this does not necessarily mean people are immobilised within that identity. The reciprocity of power: 'leaves open a possibility of agency and self determination' (p.297, quoted from de Lauretis 1987: 9). In other words if one's identity is constructed through discourse and power relations, this identity can also be reconstructed (West 1997). This theoretical perspective is also being applied more frequently amongst disabled writers to their disability contexts (Corker 1999 for example).

This study has used life histories to track the ways in which men and women constructed their identities in relation to work, family and schooling. Chapters six, seven and eight demonstrated the multiplicity of power relations which both constrain and influence behaviours and attitudes amongst different social groups. This chapter explores how the various participants saw themselves as adult learners now and how their ambitions in the present linked to experiences of the past.

What aspects of themselves did the learners identify as important? And where did those images come from? The following pages show this was a complicated picture. As their social class or cultural background influenced both choice of course and aspects of the self, I shall describe them once more according to their course participation groups.

The Portside life histories, for instance, connected with the working class poverty of the pre-war years, the post 1944 Education Act and varying phases of employment and economic insecurity. People's subjectivities were constructed as a result of the discourses of their time.

Portside

Dominant forms of social exclusion are based on the outcome of ostensibly universal criteria of achievement, reflecting personal qualities efforts and attributes (Crompton and Brown 1994: 5).

The majority of learners in the Portside group referred to their learning ability in relation to three periods in time - at school, before the community courses and after those courses. Some also compared their early ambitions with current identities - as learners and individuals. Life experiences shaped their personal consciousness at every level. They were collectively influenced, for instance, by social class images such as their sense of coming from a 'working class town', with few expectations that people would go to university 'from round here'. As universities were for 'clever people' their own identities would already be informed by that sense of difference. For example, both Margaret and Graham passed the eleven plus. Yet Margaret said: 'I wasn't very bright when I went to the grammar school, you know, just average' and Graham too said: 'I was a thickun at school'. It is difficult to shake off such histories which run deep into our lives (Rutherford 1990).

In spite of the regulatory effect of the past on the present, people's sense of self proved fluid and malleable. Perceptions of their own ability would fluctuate or remain constant, depending on their interface with other discourses. Peggy's story is an example of how easily subjectivities are affected even by small interventions. Peggy positioned herself in relation to her thirteen plus success, but failure to get a grammar school place, counterpoised by her parents' expectations for her as a girl. Her consequent self descriptions oscillated between feeling 'a failure' and 'dunderbrain' to a sense that she often acted as 'an intellectual'. She even admitted to feeling 'schizophrenic' about whether she had abilities or not. Peggy was full of contradictory self images, reflecting her sense of confusion about a lost academic world which she tried to reconstruct as a teenager through part time study for O levels: 'They was only meant to be only starters you know I was meant to do more than them'; and a sense of inferiority: 'When you've only got two O levels and everybody else has got eight it still makes you a bit inferior doesn't it'. Peggy only knew one person (her public school educated husband) with eight O levels. She aligned herself as a failure alongside him, rather than her peers or local community. Nevertheless, although she positioned herself in some instances as a failure, with little confidence, she also constructed a positive self identity in relation to her current job as a hospital medical secretary. Here the power relations were clearly defined and she had the benefit of building on an employment record which helped her construct another kind of understanding about her own abilities: 'I've got a really good memory ... I'm interested in people ... me and medical matters just click'. It is interesting to note, however, that Peggy actually applied to work as a cleaner at the hospital. She was persuaded to try the secretarial post by the outgoing member of staff.

131

Peggy's earlier jobs had been factory work. This incident reveals the precariousness of identity and its dependence on how others position you in discourses. As Skeggs (1997) said of her working class women in an ethnographic study: 'The classifying of themselves depended on the classifying systems of others' (p.74).

The accumulation of both a sense of lost opportunity and confused notion of her ability to learn seemed to fuel Peggy's desire to push herself to study: 'I just can't get enough you know, I mean anybody suggests a new subject to me I'm sort of immediately interested'. But there were limits to her own desires in terms of what level of learning to reach. She never ventured outside her immediate locality and aligned herself with dominant, class-based community discourses in relation to university learning: 'I think a lot of people think that way ... just automatically assume they weren't capable'. In spite of this entrenched position, reinforced over the years, Peggy, and others, began to form a different kind of identity after the courses. She had attended one of them with local teachers, resulting in a renewed sense of self as an equal: 'It boosts your confidence in your ability a bit I think ... because I can mix and sort of understand what they are saying'. Once more she re-aligned herself with those who can, rather than those who can't. By now, however, Peggy was also struggling with another discourse - the one that constructs ageing and which also influenced Emma, Muriel and Eric: 'It's coming to the age when I find things quite hard ... sometimes it takes me a little while to maybe click on'. Peggy, therefore, was constantly re-defining herself throughout her discussions, depending on her understanding of her own relationship to dominant discourses and other people, particularly those with authority to know - like teachers, or the medical world. Margaret did have a grammar school education, though she too was not allowed to progress as far as she would have liked. But this difference in reality between 'not quite getting there' and at least having a grammar school identity may have helped to dissipate Margaret's own frustrations. She deferred most of her ambitions onto her daughters (Both hers and Peggy's children went to university), and remained less ambitious for herself: 'I'm too laid back to seek [education] out, I like it presented on a plate'; Nevertheless she too reconstructed her self image after the courses: 'I found it easier than I thought I would ... when you've been once you realise that perhaps you're more capable than you thought you were'.

Most of the Portside participants were unconfident about their ability to learn. Many were now constructing their subjectivities around discourses of ageing. They felt, for example that they perhaps learned slowly: 'I learn slowly ... I get there in the end' (Muriel, Peggy, Julie, Sheila). But as many

132

also reconstructed their personal identity in terms of ability after the course on the same lines as Margaret.

Subjectivities were often fragilely balanced between identities formed from wider social values and those developed through more immediate personal relations. The degree of mutuality between these different discourses would influence peoples' visions of themselves in multiple ways. A mere brush with a discourse out of the normal - but from someone with authority to know could have lasting impressions on how people saw themselves: 'Our different states of consciousness lead us into constructing different social worlds' (Stanley & Wise, 1993: 132).

Where the Portside participants were influenced by social constructions of age and class, many Wyrevale respondents' self images were mixed with the need to reconstitute themselves against dominant attitudes towards disability. Individual examples are offered here, to explain how both social relationships, class positioning and disability images would affect people in different ways.

Wyrevale

> Social exclusion implies that processes are at work outwith the control of the individual (Clayton 1999: 13).

The lives of most people at Wyrevale were inextricably bound by processes outside of their control. Nevertheless, Marks (1994) suggests that disabled people would give themselves inner identities beyond those offered on their behalf:

> To have a disability is to be inscribed as other ... these constructs may be incongruent with the way students with disabilities construct their own subjectivities and those of other people with disabilities (Marks 1994: 83).

Given the opportunity to describe themselves, most people on the community courses did not see disability as the main locus of their identity. This did not always mean they had a positive alternative, however. For some their self image had been created long before their disability onset. Dave for example saw himself as: 'an evil smarmy two-faced good for nothing'. He was struggling with a lifetime of negative personal images: 'I've always been uncomfortable wi' meself because I've always thought I were thick'. Joan's identity, too, had been constructed long before her disability: 'I didn't speak to a lot of people, I was very shy with me head down and that'. Phyllis was a 'very nervous child' and Susan was: 'Always not confident. I used to stand back instead of standing forward'. Mandy described herself as not intelligent but: 'I do have common sense and I'm not thick'. Henry and Susan described themselves as both a bit 'intolerant' or 'impatient', though Henry also felt he was 'loyal, sincere'. Tony, with fond memories of his grandparents but bitter memories of school, saw himself in adult learning terms as: 'A person who wants to take something in and go out and show other people that they can go and do the same thing'.

People positioned themselves very differently therefore. Whilst Dave felt he could draw on no resources to describe himself positively, Tony tried to explain himself in terms of his value to others as a carer, perhaps in contradistinction to his own sense of need or even his sense of decreased masculinity as an amputee, or perhaps in opposition to how he felt he was constructed as a school pupil. Even Joan, the quietest and least confident of all, described herself in similar terms. She said this about herself:

> I'm quite proud of meself, of what I've done in my life, what I have done for other people. I've done a lot for me own family, they were all sick and that, me husband, nursing my mum and that and meself I think I get a lot of encouragement from other people and praise for what I've done.

Skeggs' (1994) analysis of her college students would indicate that this way of seeing yourself in relation to others (subject positioning) had been a form of disciplinary power, an unconscious desire to do no wrong. It may be that Joan's self identification, along with Tony's was more complex than that. West (1997) in his analysis of Access student biographies, frequently discussed the contingency of self and its vulnerability to negative experiences. He claimed that the risk involved in self transformation for those students, to enter higher education, required a build up of positive experiences to shift the balance of power in an individual's relationship with the world:

> It is only when self becomes sufficiently strong that one can enthusiastically enter transitional space - between one's self and others ... to take risks ... The ability to ... fight back ... requires some deeper, developing and cohesive self beyond as well as within discursive relationships (p.21).

Few of the Wyrevale participants had the luxury of any such platform from which to take risks or build an image of self in relation to education, least of all Joan. Their identities were hard earned and required constant reinforcement from whatever sources they could get. Joan, whilst indeed associating herself with a gendered care role, was also seeking a means of obtaining praise from others in order to build the first stages of a positive self image.

As always, past negative or positive experiences would intersect differentially with discourses in the present. Henry had a secure middle class upbringing and farming background. He was now caught up in a discourse which disassociated masculinity from medical models of disability. The interplay of these images meant that he fluctuated between two identities. On the one hand he would see himself as authoritative and in control:

> It's very hard to convince a farmer I can assure you ... they are very realist sort of men, they don't buy anything unless they want it or it's doing them some good or something;

and feeling positive about a future return to his last job:

> I've reason to believe the firm want me back doing something ... I've still a lot left in me I think, anyway ... I haven't lost my speech ... I do try to do as much as I can myself.

On the other hand he was also internalising a sense that his disability had taken away his masculine role and made him vulnerable:

> I've lost my independence ... I'm beholden a lot to Dorothy for being my wife ... I can't walk like I used to, I can't go up and down steps ... I mean I can't drive the car can I.

Henry had been a tall, active and strong man. He was experiencing a stark contrast of discourses which were associated with different personae. This meant he was caught between a shifting, internalised balance of power between positive and negative self images. The loss of a car had a different effect on his sense of self from the others because most, apart from Paul, had never owned a car anyway. Discourses then, interplayed differently with individuals' personae, depending on their subject positioning. New discourses with power status could shape individual subjectivities in different ways again, depending on how the inner self was already constructed.

Carol presented a similar story of shattered identity, but from a different starting point. She had started life confidently enough:

135

I used to be sort of really free and easy person ... when I was young and um full of vim and um full of 'Oh I can do it' ... you know, even if I couldn't I'd say I could cause I'd try you know.

The negative influences of her doctor and school were originally offset by the public persona drawn from a grammar education and achievement at work in a social climate which had no other expectations for working class girls. This identity was fragile, however. Her constructive dismissal at work re-positioned her as a disabled person, with no confidence:

A lot of people ... they are very shy of us ... I can't write ... as soon as they know you're disabled they don't want to know nowadays ... [education] might lead to something else for some people, but not for me.

The public discourse of disability was something which many fought long and hard against, with remarkable resilience. Gillian, for instance, was physically the most disabled of all the participants by the time I met her. Yet she came from a loving and socially secure childhood where she was an accepted member of the community: 'Kids in the street ... I was one of the gang ... I mean I don't look upon myself as being handicapped'. Her struggles with negative discourses were hampered by one power relationship which dogged her sense of her own potential for most of her life. This was the negative status and expectations of special school education: 'I always felt that because I went to special school and because I never had a real good education that was my drawback ... I'd like to find out what my IQ is'. At the same time her experience at school of encouragement from some teachers shifted the balance of power sufficiently for her to construct a self image of someone with ability - especially once she had done the community courses: 'I think I'm just above average [intelligence]'; and someone who could learn: 'I really feel I could go for it now. If I don't do something now I'll never do it'.

After twelve years at Wyrevale, Gillian stopped attending. Instead she started going to the local further education college. Gillian was only one of two Wyrevale participants to make this transition. The second was Paul, though his sense of self could also build on his first aid successes. It may be that these participants were motivated to rethink their educational decision making because of the opportunity to reflect on their lives by talking to me. It may be that they were simply 'ready' to try something new. Havighurst (1972) calls this the 'teachable moment'. He felt that the right set of personal circumstances would be the motivating factor for participation. Neither Gillian nor Paul's personal circumstances seemed significantly to

136

contribute to their educational decision making at this time. In contrast, the community courses seemed to intersect with the participants' own relatively positive selves in a way which shifted their disability power relationship with others who traditionally had authority to know more than they did. Paul gave an example of how he used this newly discovered subjectivity in committee meetings: 'Since the outreach course I've been able to put points across and actually get people to listen to what I am saying, rather than look at me blank'.

The community intervention even had a significant influence on more precarious and fragile identities. Dave, for instance, said: 'I did enjoy them and they stimulated me ... made me feel better in meself'; and Susan said: 'I didn't think that I could do half of what I've done'. Where Wyrevale gave them a disabled identity, the courses enabled them to develop their non-disabled identities.

A recent ethnographic study of disabled higher education students revealed similar inherently contradictory situations of negotiating both disabled and non disabled identities on the university campus (Low 1996). Whilst students had to obtain assistance with regard to aspects of their disability, they were at the same time constantly trying to reposition themselves as students outside of the disability category. Low explores how students break through institutionalised visions of the 'normalised' disability relationship in order to give themselves individual, and different, identities. In the light of this it is significant that whilst the bulk of the Wyrevale participants' lifestyles were negotiated around a disabled identity, only Carol and Mandy ever referred to this as a part of their self image in terms of learning. When they were invited to consider their relationship with higher education, for instance, people like Henry, Dave and Susan identified class and occupational, rather than disability issues. Dave, for instance said:

Well I've been in prison and I've been in an approved school and I don't think they understand them ... I know why I talk like I do, because I came from a pit village ... every second word of mine is a swear word ... and I'd be like a sore thumb. You know, sticking out - oh look at him isn't he thick.

Even Henry felt:

They wouldn't understand my background ... if they didn't know about farming ... they would be lost a little bit unfortunately and I would be lost with them ... they are apt to speak down to you.

From these comments it is clear that the formation of a sense of self and the self's relationship to learning motivation is both individual and highly fluid. Positive interventions need reinforcement as well as recognition of the social context of difference. Continued participation is dependent on ongoing power relations which build a sufficiently strong self so that the individual can break through dominant expectations and continue to negotiate his or her own identity within the dominant culture. These perceptions were equally applicable to the Loamshire women, but in a context which meant re-negotiating their cultural, linguistic and religious identities.

Loamshire

Woollett et al (1994), in a recent survey of British born and first generation migrant women in East London, describe how Asian women construct and reconstruct their identities across generations:

> Ethnic identity is informed by specific contexts or circumstances of their lives. Women continually redefine their ethnic identity in different contexts and settings and they maintain a balance between their own and the dominant culture (p.128).

The Loamshire women were almost a generation younger than most of the Portside and Wyrevale respondents. They had all experienced migration, marriage in a foreign country, the pressures of living in a non-Muslim or non-Hindu country, the difficulties of acquiring a new language and, usually, transition into an in-law family. Alongside this they had to contend with: 'complex forms of racialised identities in colonial and postcolonial societies' (Solomos 1993: 332). Their subjectivities within these experiences would be shaped and reshaped as the women adjusted to their new environments.

In these circumstances religion was an important and stabilising connection with the identity of both culture and country. Woollett et al (1994) and Jacobson (1997) both identified the importance of religion for minority ethnic groups as a way of defining their ethnicity. Many of the Muslim participants, for instance, when asked to describe themselves, did so in Islamic terms:

As far as the Pakistani environment is concerned I've lived according to that (Sabia); .... I am committed to my faith (Aliya); ... I think one thing that struck me about my group is most of them were very religious minded (tutor Afsar).

In contrast to the Wyrevale group, the women's strong Islamic focus gave them a positive self image, irrespective of other personal circumstances:

I am a nice person, a good person ... I value others (Sanam); ... I would describe myself as ... a good person, a [good] human being (Hinaa); ... I'm happy with the way I have been up to now ... and the way in which I bring up my children (Aliya).

The indications were that Islam, at least, gave the women a sense of continuity in a changing and unclear world. Indeed Jacobson (1997) found that a sense of religious identity would remain constant across generations and provide a source of strength for young Muslims:

Religion is a more significant source of social identity for these young people than ethnicity ...(p.233) ... although within British society they are members of a relatively small and weak minority their religious beliefs and practices traverse the globe and history (p.245).

Nevertheless the community demands of such commitments would take on a more ambivalent status for some young British born Asians, as Khan revealed: 'I do find it hard to satisfy the two personas I have, Asian Muslim girl versus British teenager' (1997: 120).

The Hindu women's identification with Hinduism was not articulated so explicitly, though chapter eight showed their temple was an important community resource and focus for social cohesion.

In spite of some positive religious identities other aspects to the women's lives not only isolated them as 'different' but also affected their confidence. An issue which touched every one of the Asian participants, for instance, was the impact on their self image of trying to communicate in English. Compared with the self confidence of their religious personae, the women were uneasy in their unfamiliar and unequal power relationship with those who spoke English. Not being able to understand or speak English would have a range of negative effects on people's understanding of their place in the world, irrespective of perceived identities outside of that context. Madhun, for instance, with a successful degree from India, said this: 'In front of English people I feel so dull, so thick really because I'm not able to communicate'. Sanam, a teacher in Pakistan, would avoid areas where she needed to speak English: 'I'm afraid that if I speak and I speak broken English people are going to laugh at me'. Their imprisonment, already environmentally apparent, now became social as well.

Some women managed to move beyond this perceived state of disempowerment and develop a new kind of personal agency (self determination). On occasions this was through necessity, resulting from changed circumstances. Ruksana, for instance, the least educated of all, reconstituted a different gender relationship with her husband compared with the other women because he could speak less English than herself. The dynamics of this relationship gave her a new role:

> I'm supporting my husband so I have to learn to speak and look after myself. I'm actually educated more than him although my education is very limited. My English is better than his so if my children ever need to go to hospital or any appointments I actually take them and talk.

As with the other groups, the women's shifts in identity or sense of agency depended on the balance of power at any given time, rather than any sense of fixed self image or background. As subjectivities could shift so could power relations.

On another occasion for instance the women's awareness of their unequal power relationships, caused by language differences, would even stimulate anger. The anger could derive from different identities. For Hinaa it was her realisation of how unconfident she had become:

> I think it [lack of confidence] really started to change when I was angry with myself for being like this and for letting people get the better of me and that really made me want to change (Hinaa);

Shivani, too, reacted to a story of belittling experiences on arrival in England. She had survived her first few days in the country with the help of a cardboard hand which relatives in India had given her. This had written on it a request for a translator. Shivani's humiliating memory of how much she needed the hand and how helpless she had felt on arrival alone at the airport gave her a particular goal:

> I felt frustrated, I felt angry, I felt guilty that I couldn't communicate and that really made me determined to learn English. I felt really bad, I felt was I really that bad that I needed something like that hand to help me get through?

140

In spite of these examples of self-generated agency, the hegemonic effect of being a member of the Indian Sub Continent in colonial Britain had a significant power effect on all these women. It is hard to imagine an English person's identity being subject to those feelings in India or Pakistan for instance. There are some similarities between these experiences and those described by the tutors Lesley and Mavis in relation to disability. Mavis and Lesley, from their privileged middle class positions, identified a particular, self-perpetuating disability power relationship with the 'normal world' which would affect one's whole being. As Mavis said:

> The whole process of acquiring a disability does produce very negative feelings which have got nothing to do with how they felt about themselves before ... it's the way you are treated by other people.

Subjectivities, then, are manipulated by the power of dominant discourses which construct difference as 'other' and unequal. Only Aliya ever articulated the contradiction of feeling inferior because you can't speak English, even though you could speak at least two other languages fluently, and the English could communicate in neither of them. Aliya also realised the extent to which some women's fear of not coping with English would undermine them so much so that they would not even attend English classes: 'I think they are apprehensive more than anything else. I think they are worried that they are going to be clamped down on and that's why they come and leave'.

But as earlier stories have shown, even these anxieties can be traced to earlier experiences, which - if reinforced in the present- can resurrect a negative identity which may once have disappeared. Conversely, positive early memories could give people strength to sustain themselves through current negative experiences. Sanam suggested that teachers in Pakistan, in her experience, would often only encourage children who were already achieving. The memories of the women who talked to Afsar and Kajal suggest that many of them had been successful students in school. So, where neo colonialism helped to engender one form of subjectivity, Loamshire participants seemed to draw on positive images of their ability to learn, irrespective of whether they had reached their achievement goals. All claimed they had been encouraged at school and at home, resulting in a sense of learning potential which neither of the other two groups could match. As Afsar said of her group: 'Most of them do think they have the ability to learn. I don't think any of them has been knocked back by anybody'. Aliya and Hinaa each regarded themselves as 'a good student'. Many felt anything was possible if the will was there. The following comment was typical: 'No matter what stage of life you are in if you work hard and if you're dedicated you can achieve absolutely anything' (Hinaa). Sara, for instance, age 25 by the first interview, with four children and married at sixteen, had ample proof of her academic potential:

> I actually was a year ahead so I did two years' education in one year, in effect, so I matriculated at fourteen ... If I hadn't got married I would definitely have gone to college and I would hopefully have graduated.

In spite of fragile identities regarding the English language, they would therefore be able to draw on past successes to recreate enough self esteem to move forward in England. Aliya's comment was typical: 'I want to stand on my own two feet, I want to be independent ... so that I can sort out my own problems'. Similarly for Sara, the community intervention - if coupled with a discourse which aligned itself with her own required study constraints - re-positioned Sara's sense of herself as someone who might still become a graduate:

> Yes I still want to [study], I still think of it, especially after doing this course ... I know that [local, franchised study] is possible now and it has actually given me hope that I could still be a student at a university.

In this respect the Loamshire women contradicted a common association of social exclusion with low self esteem, alienation and disillusionment (Clayton 1999: 114). This indicates that exclusion is defined by the colonisers, rather than the colonised. The isolating process of exclusion itself could have an effect of destabilising the self - but this depended on how other power and agency factors interlinked (Mulgan 1998).

These stories show that neither social exclusion nor their related identities are fixed or inevitable states. But the reproduction of certain power relations and their associated discourses could perpetuate the exclusion of difference. Resultant subjectivities would be determined by a range of factors. Multiple identities, how people positioned themselves in different social situations and their sometimes contradictory selves all formed their subjective self, but as part of the social relations in which they were placed:

> Identity is not simply an individual matter but a social product located in time and space. It is not a fixed static entity but has to be seen as a dynamic process (Allen 1994: 90).

It is the dynamic nature of subjectivity which is key to how learners, and therefore the socially excluded, are constructed, rather than construct themselves. Whilst the Loamshire women as: 'The perceived transmitters of cultural values and identities' (Afshar 1994: 130); wandered uneasily in an unfamiliar society, many would struggle to find social cohesion in cultural and religious practices which might nevertheless have the power effect of excluding them further from dominant discourses irrespective of their potential or motivation. A few would feel able to recreate new identities in a different set of power dynamics. So Madhun and Shivani talked ambitiously of wanting careers in their new country:

> To get a job which I enjoy that's very important, my career is very important, to get a job with job satisfaction ... I would like to become a clerical officer or administration officer in a college or university, so that's my ambition (Madhun).

By the end of the study Madhun did indeed obtain an administration job in her local college. But compared with the other participants, she was drawing on substantial cultural capital from India.

The Asian women's lives were torn between a need to retain an identity which valued their religion and cultural heritage and a desire to feel integrated in a society which already constructed them as inferior. Each found her own way of forging identities which had to accommodate such a world. As for Portside and Wyrevale, the intersection of new discourses and their power effect on old discourses would be critical in deciding how the women would engage with educational provision in this country.

This chapter has shown that dominant images of class, disability, ethnicity, gender and age would all influence the individual's inner sense of self. The unpredictability and precariousness of identity, however, is more fragile for people whose lifeworlds are furthest from the idealised norm. How people contest normative images depends on a number of interlocking factors. For example whilst past experiences of positive identities might sometimes enable individuals to forge new identities in negative circumstances this would depend on the balance of power in that context:

> Identity as a dynamic aspect of social relationships is forged and reproduced through the agency/structure dyad and is inscribed within unequal power relationships ... identity is not one thing for any individual ... each individual is ... located ... in a number of different and at times conflictual identities (Bhavnani & Phoenix 1994: 9).

143

The issue here is how to offset the effect of negative and unequal power relationships to build a positive sense of self and cultivate learning potential.

These last four chapters have dissected different aspects of the learners' life histories. In the process I hope I have shown both the complexity of building a positive learner identity but also the myriad insights which are simply not recognised as knowledge within the hierarchy of academia. The cumulative effect of labelling people according to an external reference point - as well as then subjugating the very knowledge which is privileged to their social circumstances results in educational social exclusion. Excluding the socially excluded not only has wider economic consequences but it also deprives the mainstream of diversity and new ways of looking at old problems. The dominant pattern of inclusion by normalisation has not worked. It is therefore time to look at new solutions to old problems. The final two chapters will summarise the main issues from this study and make suggestions for a more inclusive and richer kind of higher education fit for a learning society.

10 Combating social exclusion re-assessed

Social exclusion is commonly associated with poverty and absence from the labour market (Oppenheim 1998, Clayton 1999). Few of the participants in this book were even registered as seeking work and even fewer were in work. An education system therefore which associates participation primarily with the labour market is in danger of making invisible those who are already excluded. Moreover, the stories of these individual learners indicate that the picture of participation and exclusion, in educational terms, is more complicated than a purely economic analysis might suggest (Brine 1999).

Educational decision making results from a multiplicity of interlinked factors. Certain social groups receive mixed messages about what they are entitled to. Perceptions of who you are and what you can do are influenced by attitudes and behaviours from across people's lives. Provision which prescribes a narrow curriculum and fixed outcomes can make those same groups feel invisible and marginalised. Attempts to widen participation amongst those already excluded therefore needs to take their values and experiences into account. Their perspectives often challenge the dominant curriculum and style of provision. Such findings raise the question: Who has authority to know and what counts as valuable knowledge?

This chapter looks at the case for challenging current practices in university continuing education. It revisits some of the arguments outlined across the book. I look at the contrasting academic positions on standards, appropriateness, teaching and the academic curriculum. I then show how those most on the margins responded to educational opportunities at various points in their lives; how some struggled to invest in learning experiences which meant something to them and how an accumulation of attitudes over time would ultimately define their sense of entitlement.

It would not be possible, in one project, to cover all parts of the education system. The focus of this particular study is on the most flexible aspect of higher education - part time continuing education. Chapter one looked at recent literature which is beginning to question some of the fundamental principles behind higher education which define its elite status and protect it from difference in the name of 'excellence'. I raised questions about higher education's criteria for excellence, the specific relationship between critical analysis and text, the notion of an adult learner as a certain type of autonomous individual, the idea of an appropriate curriculum for higher education, the concept of impartiality embedded in the higher education system.

In chapter one I claimed that universities have played a particular role in putting forward certain forms of knowledge at the expense of others. Their success in delegitimising working class attempts at alternative ways of knowing, for example, is documented by historians (Fieldhouse 1996, Simon 1990). The legacy of the university's representation of its own version of 'neutral', 'impartial' but 'critical' knowledge creation is also documented in the literature (Barnett 1990, Fieldhouse 1985, Robbins 1963). Attempts to compromise university modes of inquiry so that they accommodate those most on the margins also have a long history (Fordham et al 1979, Ward & Taylor 1986, Jackson 1980, Lovett 1982, for example). Arguments have consistently maintained that universities do not speak to ordinary people and that the curriculum needs to be broadened and viewed differently for wider participation to take place (Ball 1990).

There are new trends to this debate, however. Recent thinking suggests that a mass higher education system need to re-focus its 'higher' levels of thinking onto learning processes, rather than teaching content. So the idea of learning 'adaptability' skills has been promoted by some as a way forward (McNair 1998, Watson and Taylor 1998); but also challenged by others as another form of surveillance designed to produce lifelong learners: 'Who will readily police themselves in the service of an advanced capitalist economy' (Edwards 1999: 265). Furthermore this study showed that a change of teaching process alone may not be enough to engage the disaffected or marginalised. The fundamental relationship behind those processes needs to be questioned. One aspect of this relationship is explained in chapter two. There I argued that dominant values are sustained by subordinating alternative values. Social conditioning creates an unequal balance of power which affects the way people elevate certain kinds of knowledge and understanding. The consequence is to hierarchise the people who are carriers of those forms of knowledge and understanding. The difficulty is that we all collude in delegitimating different perspectives and in arguing for the status quo. The familiar usually appears to be the most common sense. The discourse of appropriateness, for instance, is a particularly effective institutional mechanism for fencing in the nuances of acceptable academic behaviour (Fairclough 1992a).

Real inclusion must give voice to those delegitimated discourses. In order to explain why this must happen it was necessary to unearth some of

146

the deeply embedded roots of what higher education stands for. Chapters three and four looked at some practices within higher education which directly affected its continuing education activity and impinged on community education work. In these chapters people justified, for example, the existing neutrality of university education as a defence against new curricula or tutors. Explanations for value-free curricula and quality were expressed as a self-referencing procedure of peer review. So if those already in the institution agreed with the curriculum content then it must already be perfect. The strategies in place to monitor quality comprised of systems which had already delegitmated difference as less than what was already on offer. Consequently commitment to widening participation has been articulated in a climate which sees no real need for change within the institution. If change does occur it is still against particular reference points against which future directions for change are judged. So, for example, subject content could only be recognised within the institution's existing disciplines. Chapters three and four showed these were supported by the use of certain words such as (text based) critical analysis and reference to approved bibliographies. These words had their own internalised meanings. They were discourses which had a power relationship with other discourses. Their effectiveness was most apparent when people were asked to consider deviations from the norm. For example, it became difficult to consider studying topics in any other form than through text ('What are they operating with if there isn't a text?' LA2). So subject matter, such as family history, is not acceptable because it does not use the language of particular disciplines. Decisions to exclude therefore were based on the adoption of certain words and meanings ('I don't think genealogy is a university subject' - LA1) or with reference to 'the institution' as a frame of reference ('There have been instances when we've fallen foul of the institution' - HOD3 ... 'The university is looking over our shoulder' - CA1). The ability of these power systems to travel across universities and departments was demonstrated when academic staff from four different institutions shared similar strategies, language and rationalities for sustaining or excluding certain practices.

The next few sections in this chapter summarise how power defines and excludes through discourse. The combination of particular features of difference resulted in the social exclusion of learners without authority to learn. Later sections, however, look at how those power relations can be altered to facilitate social inclusion which celebrates difference.

Specific themes running through the study were the status of text and curriculum. The written word, for example, was an especially powerful and self defining discourse in the university institution.

147

The social situation of text and words

Perhaps the most remarkable example of how words take on their own meaning and become 'socially situated' (Fairclough 1995), was when I attempted to intervene in the development of a blues course. In this instance the boundaries for understanding curriculum content could only be articulated through the language of disciplinarity. The more emotive curriculum issues of slavery and black feminism, though written down on the page as such, were subliminated under the more 'neutral' notion of a music course, in order to defend the status of a white tutor. Challenges to perceived normality were then interpreted as deviant and threatening to the status quo. It appeared that difference can only be integrated if it is managed by people who don't acknowledge the features of difference itself. This anomaly was expressed in one way or another by all the community higher education staff who consistently identified quality in terms of differential learner values in preference to 'fitting in'. For community staff the curriculum had to be relevant to the learners, not necessarily the institutional infrastructures.

Curriculum relevance for the learner

> Top down programmes can look impressive on paper but simply won't work if local communities do not share ownership and responsibility (Mulgan 1998: 266).

A principle argument for new mechanisms of social inclusion is that the marginalised themselves must have a voice in their own affairs. The community staff also talked about an appropriate curriculum. But they did so from a starting point which already assumed a position of neutrality was impossible. The community curriculum was overtly applied differentially in order to engage with learner standpoints. Quality and level, therefore, took on new meanings in these different contexts. It was quality of insight which was important, not which standpoint and which text book was used. Inevitably this strategy produced new insights, albeit less authoritative (the Wyrevale group's response to their video about a wheelchair user's day for example).

Whilst such efforts demonstrated the potential for including difference within the curriculum, the participants themselves revealed a much more complicated personal profile regarding education and participation. Several lifelong factors would mitigate against producing simple solutions. The

148

idea of entitlement, for instance, an automatic notion for those with cultural capital, had long since been rationalised away amongst the working classes. The same intricate process of giving only certain meanings to words resulted in the privileging of the privileged and denial of those not entitled. There began to emerge stories of differential treatment with regard to education, work and social space.

Confusing truths and colluding with exclusion

Chapters six and seven were the first chapters to privilege the learners' voices. In doing so they revealed the complexity of truth and the complexities against which people struggle to make their realities fit the mainstream view of their surrounding world. So dominant perspectives for class, gender and disability would justify why people did not need to take up those educational opportunities to which the middle classes or male counterparts were entitled. The discourses were so widespread amongst the professionals who distributed educational opportunities that even those on the receiving end would eventually believe and accept their destiny. I showed in chapter six how a combination of political and economic goals on behalf of the privileged world materialise into justifications which keep the rest in their place. So the individual learners would recall how schools, parents and employers colluded in educational decision making processes. It was only when the learners tried to piece together arguments which justified their exclusion at the time ('There were plenty of jobs around .. you didn't need qualifications') alongside perceived realities of the time ('The choice was very limited for girls' - Peggy; ... 'It took me two years to get a job' - Gillian); that we begin to realise that something else is happening with these discourses. The discourses are part of a power relationship between the dominant power holders - those with authority to know - and those whose voice is delegitimated. The effect of such discourses, however, was to prove long lasting. New rationalities for maintaining the status quo would be reproduced over time. The learners would internalise their own exclusion and no longer seek to resist ('That's what all the people closest to me thought, so I thought the same' - Peggy).

For the Loamshire women, Eastern truths, reason and meaning were even more sharply contrasted against Western ideologies. So the women would struggle to reinterpret their sense of entitlement to Western space ('This country's like a prison' - Afsar). They would then try and understand the values of education in a world whose criteria for learning were almost in opposition to Eastern religions and cultures ('My parents were afraid I would become westernised and go astray' - Ruksana).

By chapter seven the effect of such collusions across race, class, gender and culture was overwhelming. Reinforced by those with authority to know and often inveigled in the discourse of 'care', the individual learners found their own rationales for dismissing the value of their own insights and quality of their ways of knowing. Where several generations were involved, attitudes of the past impinged on attitudes of the present. Education for those already excluded in the past was not seen as a ticket to anywhere in the present ('It might lead somewhere for some people, but not for me' - Carol). Similarly across the participant generations people stated they were either too old to study, intelligence belonged to a different generation or education would lead you astray.

The learner groups were enmeshed in different webs of power which, for many, resulted in a form of self surveillance. Dominant attitudes and values were reproduced across generations and by professionals. People maintained the social order - at the expense of any inner desires. Often their apparent acceptance of the status quo was the cumulative result of unrewarded resistances throughout their lives. Yet their adult learner status, as defined in the literature, required a pro-active self-directing approach to education (Knowles 1990). But for several individuals in this story, their struggles for a pro-active position in society had already absorbed considerable energy, perhaps disproportionate to the gains achieved. Gillian's story of her childhood attempt to prove her capability at riding a two wheeler bike and her repeated efforts as a teenager to find a way past restrictive employment rules demonstrate this point.

Similarly the new discourses of inclusion and exclusion are in danger of ignoring the recognition that exclusion is socially constructed. Individualistic solutions for example have a tendency to promote integration as 'normalisation'. For some the difficulties of breaking out of their category of social exclusion are caused in part by the very discourses for social inclusion. What counts as worthwhile 'social capital' for example is not a neutral concept. In the same way that family history was reinscribed by the history lecturer 'genealogy', equality is also being reinscribed in terms of human capital values. So as Brine (1999) suggests:

The outcomes of equality policies remain the same - that is only exceptional or fortunate individuals from the ranks of the long term unemployed will gain access to (relatively secure, full time) employment and become part of the socially included (p.69).

Systems for education and training therefore are constructed around these values.

In spite of this bleak picture, chapters eight and nine showed that this situation is not inevitable. Aside from addressing some of the more practical concerns for study, the principle features of the community courses were that they recognised knowledge on differential terms and attempted to address people's sense of self. Neither strategy was simple, embedded as they were in already unequal power relationships and systems which already privileged cultural capital. Only a few examples are mentioned here. Undoubtedly more could be found in the lives of different individuals.

Knowledge on our terms

The image of 'non participant' is compounded by dominant meanings attached to 'education'. In chapter eight the participants demonstrated new ways of knowing and different forms of critical thinking. Change the criteria for defining education and you include new learners. People did undertake learning activities. But sometimes the significance of these activities was not recognised because they did not fit the authorised definition of learning, curriculum or even who counts as a learner. For instance, many of the Loamshire women learned English through watching television - a practice undervalued by Schuller and Bostyn (1993) in their analysis of informal learning activities. Similarly women from Portside drew on their family roles to gain critical insights, even though they disregarded them as part of their own store of knowledge. The dominant discourses for higher education, moreover, would disregard much community learning organised by staff like myself. Although such provision contained elements of higher education ideology, it still lay outside the boundaries of university norms for 'level', 'quality' or 'curriculum'.

There were ways of mediating knowledge on the participants' terms. These related in this study to the cultural and social values of gender, disability, class and religious consciousness; a consciousness which desired educational experiences to be meaningful in the context of people's lives. This kind of education was managed and filtered by the role model tutors and link workers. So for Karen progression had to be decided by the learners, not by some externally imposed criteria: 'What they did with that knowledge was up to them'. For the Loamshire women learning was single sex and in a congenial location, with topics taught in a way which recognised and valued their cultural and religious background ('I have to

151

make a conscious effort of applying it to the Asian family' - Afsar) and for Wyrevale, disability perspectives were an inclusive part of their critical thinking ('If they put a drop kerb for instance it's not just helping a wheelchair user ... its helping a blind person with a stick' - Paul). These teaching and learning experiences have some similarity to Aronowitz and Giroux's (1991) notion of border pedagogy. Aronowitz and Giroux advocate the privileging of different kinds of knowledge - where teaching shifts from transmission of prescribed knowledge to one which includes a deeper recognition of learner context. In this respect Aronowitz and Giroux's border pedagogy provides the philosophical framework within which the courses developed. The practical approach to each course, however, was influenced by the tutor's own understanding of the learners, the nature of the topic under discussion and the interaction with the learners themselves. The significant feature of each course was the recognition of subjugated or situated knowledge (Preece 1997, 1999) and individual subjectivities so that: 'Learning and achievement therefore addressed different states of adulthood' (Preece 1997a: 6). The teaching was not necessarily framed by anti-racist strategies advocated by many protagonists of transformative or radical pedagogies (hooks 1994, for example). Nevertheless, the practice of using role models ensured insider perspectives and respect for where people were coming from. These aspects of community learning challenged the common assumption that they are simply a first stage in the learning progression ladder, as the following paragraphs show.

Learning on our terms

Learning on the learners' terms meant that learning pace was not linked to a fixed notion of learning achievement. A significant feature for many of the participants was a sense that their learning was not a pressurised experience ('We weren't rushed like we are on mainstream courses' - Paul) Similarly, whilst the courses in this study were not accredited, the option of gaining credit, as identified in the academic review extract (chapter three), was built into the community courses, but within a framework of flexible content, finish and start times. The discourse of learner achievement therefore was reconstructed to allow space for the learner voice (Williams 1998).

So learning and knowledge were always contextualised. Quality was not predicated on approved bibliography lists or patterns of study. Broader issues were included, but they were raised in ways which made connections with people's lives. So study could be relatively subject specific, such as the family history courses, or it might draw on knowledge from within the learners because no text had ever authorised that knowledge (as in Wyrevale's case). Their common denominator was that their learning took place outside higher education's normative boundaries for discipline based knowledge. Boundaries were set by the learners and tutors together. They included recognition of emotion and experience as valid parts of the teaching material. The teaching and learning experience would develop insights and comparisons, a desire to go on learning and a critical spirit within that broader framework.

Alongside these strategies were the now well argued aspects of community courses which make up the social fabric of such learning environments. So concepts of mutuality (no pressure) and acceptance of each other all contributed to bel hook's version of engaged pedagogy - which would affirm people's presence and right to speak.

The solution is not that simple of course. Continuing education might well decide to engage with more flexible curricula and re-invest in the liberal tradition of negotiated learning. These approaches however, would still be competing with more institutionally grounded discourses. People's sense of 'otherness' has been determined from many corners and their willingness to participate now is heavily invested in a mixture of past experiences and current expectations. Chapter nine revealed some of the ways in which people build up a sense of themselves as learners. The extent to which they succeeded in nurturing their learning potential would depend on a multiplicity of circumstances.

Creating a strong enough sense of self

> Identities which are socially and/or linguistically constructed are open to reconstruction (West 1997: 210).

It is the very contingency of self and its susceptibility to power relations which makes learner motivation and self belief so hard to sustain. It is also the contingency of self and its vulnerability to discourses which creates the possibility for change and the development of an agency of self. As West (1997) points out, however, this can only be achieved after sufficient build up of positive experiences to trigger and sustain the risk involved in stepping into new terrains and new discourses. For many of the participants in this study the community intervention simply opened the potential of such possibilities. The stage which their own identity reached during this process depended on past life histories and was reflected in their self images as learners. So for Dave the community courses: 'made me feel better in meself', but for Sanam, with a family background of higher education and having achieved her O levels a year early, ability to learn was linked more to an awareness of what might be possible in her cultural environment: 'I now know that local study is possible now and it has actually given me hope that I could still be a student at a university'. In either case a process of self awareness had begun to shift the balance of power for future interventions, provided they were not offset by other power relationships in the meantime. Their perspectives on what kind of higher education learning environment they might enter, however, was heavily influenced by their existing experience of the community programme.

In the majority of cases the community courses did two things. They shifted ordinary people's perceptions of 'the university' and its potential for including difference. The intervention also provided an opportunity for people to develop their critical thinking skills. This meant applying them to new contexts as well as articulating existing critical abilities in ways which were relevant and purposeful to themselves: ('We're talking to family members ... now encouraging people to tell stories which are never written down' - Graham). The multiplicity and fragmentation of their potential identities, however, meant they were subject to competing power relations. Self images were also shaped by the meanings they themselves attached to discourses. The connections which they made between different combinations of familiar, and less familiar, educational experiences would help determine future participation in learning and how that learning would be developed. The validation of their learner identities in this process meant that some at least could sufficiently re-position themselves in relation to the wider educational power systems to foster further engagement in the formal system. Others continued to study outside that system but on their terms. This kind of observation has implications, of course, for future models of university adult education. Embracing the multiplicities of learner diversity and difference means challenging the status quo and also being open to constant change thereafter. The final chapter looks at these implications for future higher education policy, but there are also messages for broader concepts of lifelong learning in the context of an inclusive society.

11 Conclusions and recommendations

> It is a necessary feature of mass higher education systems ... that previous elite forms must change (Jary & Parker 1999: 5).

The new discourse for widening participation has come about because of globalisation and technological change. There is now an economic imperative to produce a workforce which can respond to a fast changing world and be mobile across different nationalities. The discourse of equal opportunities is therefore predicated on a political response to global competition and capitalism. The third speed population (Saad 1997), which is not part of this human capital, is not economically viable. But measures to address this issue currently derive their meaning for social inclusion from economic premises (Vandenbroucke 1998). Notions of social justice and plurality are not concerns of the modern world.

There are risks in this kind of economic discourse and alternative arguments need to be nurtured. For instance, if the third speed (those not economically active) remain disenfranchised from the new participation initiatives, one of two things can happen. On the one hand their voices may be silenced by the economic discourse which claims to be speaking on their behalf. One effect of this might be that their needs are discredited to pave the way for political decisions which remove them as a dependent economic burden from the global economy. The state abdicates responsibility for them. Alternatively an economic argument can be found to justify a different form of inclusion - one predicated on social capital (Schuller 1997, 1998) - but a form of social capital which takes a broader view of the features of social life currently being recognised in the literature. This would see the underlying values articulated by the learners in this study as part of a different economy. For instance, the Loamshire women's planned investment for their own children, the Wyrevale group's reduced dependency on social and other public services, the Portside group's re-creation of a cultural heritage which might have economic value for future generations. The role of higher education in building such social capital is to recognise new frontiers of knowledge and their social contexts to look at alternatives to the failed 'trickle down' formula of capitalist approaches to economic equality. This is not to say that proposed new systems for participation are all inappropriate - simply they are inadequate to address the whole picture.

Chapter ten identified six features of higher education learning in a community context. Firstly a comparison of traditional modes with community education styles exposed how certain words relating to higher education quality are context bound, rather than simply value-free or neutral. Secondly I argued that the concept of curriculum relevance needs to acknowledge and incorporate the social context of learners into the curriculum itself, in order to stimulate new insights and frontiers for knowledge. Thirdly 'exclusion' was revealed as the responsibility of all aspects of society. Everyone has contributed to the discourses which have kept people in an unequal power relationship with those with authority to know. To affect real inclusion requires a multi-faceted approach. We need new discourses that speak on behalf of the marginalised but which hold political and economic authority to ensure change comes about. Because truth is a construction it can be re-constructed if the political will is there. Fourthly knowledge requires a broader, and more inclusive, set of curriculum boundaries than those defined by higher education. Knowledge is more than scientific exposition or information; it is also about interrelationships and understanding of different levels of consciousness as opposed to depth of reading. Fifthly learning goals and achievements should be set in the context of individual learning pace, rather than fixed time limits.

Sixthly, but by no means least, notions of the adult learner should be reconstituted with an awareness of the relationship between the sense of self and ability to learn. In other words the learning self may have to be nurtured against many contradictory voices before the learner has sufficient personal agency to know and recreate their own energy to learn autonomously. An assumption that the autonomous self is where the higher education learner starts from will deny the learning potential of many socially excluded individuals.

The time is now ripe to argue for change. There is a growing policy commitment to mass higher education and a perception by some at least that the vast majority (Ball, 1990 stated 95%) of people could benefit from higher education. The call for higher education to transform how it sees itself in the domain of a mass higher education world and discourse for lifelong learning is now well rehearsed (Schuller 1995, Nixon 1996, Scott 1997, Coffield 1996, Coffield & Williamson 1997, Williamson 1998, Jary & Parker 1999). Much of these discussions hinge around the relationship between higher education and the rest of society (Coffield 1996a,

Williamson 1996, 1998). Williamson (1998) argues that universities should embrace the idea of a 'learning democracy' where new systems embrace diversity and a wider range of interests which interface with societal changes. This means, he argues, changing the infrastructure of how the university organisation functions - so that it is seen to be of immediate value to the public at large. There is also a school of thought which argues that these kinds of demands for a new higher education are better met if higher education is seen as a philosophy of learning, rather than a place to learn. Tuckett (1996) for example argues that higher education should be a: 'Kind of education: defined by the ways in which it combines the creation and transmission of knowledge rather than by its role in social selection'. He asks for a curriculum framework which pays:

> Attention to issues which underpin a plural, tolerant learning society; and: teaching approaches which build on the practical experience of learners, as well as established bodies of knowledge and current research (p.48).

More recently McNair (1998) has taken these ideas further. In recognition that the future lifelong learner will be a mature adult, not an 18 to 21 year old, he claims that teaching should recognise adults more specifically. Learning and teaching therefore is a process of knowledge creation, rather than of knowledge transmission. Teachers and learners would then need a different kind of relationship - one where they work together to make meaning. These proposals alone, however, would not necessarily address the fundamental issue that higher education needs to exchange its traditional ivory image for a more integrative role with the wider social world. The evidence in this study shows that higher education needs to develop additional responsibilities which embrace a broader notion of inclusiveness and integration (informed by research) with those on the margins of society's dominant norms. Stimulating the idea of university study comes about through intervention and dialogue. Retaining new university students requires recognition of their intrinsic value to a learning democracy. Furthermore, as the community learners showed, the development of marginalised learner identities is fragile and unpredictable. The acquisition of learning relationships which move from acquiring knowledge to the process of critical thinking valued by higher education is not necessarily linear or sequential. Whilst the public message is that underrepresented groups must be encouraged to participate in higher education, the assumption is that new learners will be expected to 'adapt' to the constraints of an existing system rather than contribute new ways of thinking and knowing.

The difficulty in defining a new higher education in any explicit terms is that it is difficult to move beyond the already exclusionary behaviours of those who have defined the system so far. It is also difficult to go to the other extreme and create a higher education system based entirely on outsider views. The very exclusion of outsiders - as the research shows - often denies them a foundation from which to construct any useful meaning of higher education. The compromise position, then, is to use the perspectives of existing critics and link them with those few available experiences of socially excluded voices. This combination, I would argue moves the debate on from the proposals by Tuckett and others, but still uses a framework which captures the essence of the lifelong learning ideal as a 'continuum' (Skilbeck & Connell 1996: 57). It also incorporates a skills development approach advocated by Wagner and others: 'By which individuals develop the capability to adjust to the uncertainties of their life experience' (Wagner 1996: 67). Skilbeck and Connell suggest these skills should include the following:

- 'an enquiring mind', inclusive of a critical spirit;
- 'helicopter vision', incorporating an understanding of breadth and interconnectedness of knowledge;
- 'information literacy' including an ability to locate, resource, retrieve and critically evaluate information;
- 'a sense of personal agency' and self awareness of one's own strengths and weaknesses (1996: 57-8).

It might be argued that these goals have as much relevance to further education (FE) as to higher education. Indeed, it may be that FE needs to shift its own boundaries beyond the mainly instrumentalist approach to learning promoted by FE funders. However, for a new kind of higher education to be effective on a long term basis it needs to change attitudinally, not just its structural framework. The most explicit arguments for such change come from anti-racist literature (Leicester 1993, Brah 1992, for example). One example of the implications for such change comes from Bonnett. She advocates a self critical exploration of one's own (white) identity. By exploring this relatively unchallenged identity, she argues, people can begin to recognise the potential for change and pluralism, as opposed to the commonly perceived position of being either 'white' or 'other' (Bonnett 1996). Debates are not confined to antiracist perspectives, of course, as recent writers on social class issues demonstrate (Lynch & O'Riordan 1998). The same strategy should also apply to disability, age, sexuality and gender. A change of focus from the analysis of 'otherness' onto the unchallenged 'self' raises the possibility of seeing power relationships as multi-dimensional. I argue for two strategies to address the issue of radical attitudinal change.

Firstly there is a need for more research into aspects which are only touched on in this study. For instance, further investigation is required into alternative curriculum and teaching models. We need more evidence about the student experience, the effectiveness of different student guidance and support systems, how students respond to learning which addresses cultural or other insider perspectives, the effect of role model teaching on the learner's sense of self and the impact of accrediting different ways of knowing. In Foucault's terms, this would mean addressing how teacher status is differentiated, and the criteria which define good teaching. The rationalities for certain activities would inevitably alter; and in order to ensure their appropriateness within the institution's framework, its management (committee) structure and surveillance systems (rules of behaviour) would require an inclusive and pluralistic membership. Quality assurance criteria would have to acknowledge, for example, values which are currently outside the boundaries of the existing academic fraternity and a consideration of which perspectives the curriculum is challenging or including. We need, for instance, a better understanding of social capital. In relation to this we also need more in-depth analysis of the shared networks and values which make up the social fabric of marginalised groups. This will give us a more informed understanding of how to generate participation as well as advocate higher education responses to the sector's regional and other democratic responsibilities advocated by Williamson.

The structuring of consequent institutional ways of behaving would impinge on how higher education delivers its own 'kind of learning' within and outside the institution. For instance there needs to be a re-examination of the systems which underpin higher education values. The following list offers some examples for change which maintain the spirit of higher education as advocated above, but within a different value system. These aspects might form the basis for change:

- Critical analysis should recognise subjugated (experiential) knowledge as a reference point for developing new knowledge. There should be opportunity to question the existing systems for knowledge making, so that the higher education way of doing things is not taken for granted.
- This means accepting that knowledge does not represent universal truths. It is valid for certain social groups, and also context bound. It would also not necessarily be discipline specific in its contribution to

159

ways of knowing and doing. In order to capture the broader framework for such knowledge creation, new ways of recording and recognising knowledge should be sought - so that Muriel's counselling experiences and Paul's disability awareness are integral to, and sources for, authoritative knowledge. These experiences would also lead to a more multi-dimensional understanding of the social networks which contribute to the validation of such ways of knowing.

- People should be allowed to learn at differential speeds. This means there would be greater emphasis on achievement rather than time bound entry and end points. Such a process should include accreditation systems which address more flexible assessment criteria (Merton 1997, Preece 1997b) than the current national qualifications framework is proposing (Wilson 1999).
- The implications of such learning would mean that end goals are not solely credited in linear mode and may relate to social as well as individual purpose. This latter feature would then accommodate the central aspect of much community education - but now within a framework which enables social purpose to be a criterion for quality in terms of generating citizenship skills and outcomes (Taylor 1997).
- Teaching should actively involve staff from more diverse backgrounds to reflect the wider social make up of society. It would be hoped that from this the teaching experience itself would include a more proactive awareness of learner identities and their potential.

All the above have in some way been addressed in this book. For example, end goals and linearity were challenged by Karen who saw that what you did with your knowledge was up to you. The formation of a family history society or extended learning into different subjects were all unaccreditable learning achievements. Similarly, almost all the participants started their learning journey at different levels of achievement and all valued the opportunity to learn at their own pace. The strategy of learning which embraces experiential, contextualised and non discipline specific knowledge has already been argued (chapter eight, for example).

Higher education institutions, then, need to address a wider range of issues than hitherto if they are to embrace social inclusion as part of university learning. Such a process takes time and requires ongoing engagement with minority groups through learning programmes which forefront the minority voice. This does not say that all text based and discipline specific knowledge has no place in the postmodern future. It does highlight, however, the contingent and power-driven basis on which such learning has held its exclusionary, authoritative status. Inclusive education recognises difference and the relationships which make up the lives of different social groups.

Bibliography

Abberley P (1987) The Concept of Oppression and the Development of a Social Theory of Disability, *Disability Handicap and Society* 2 (1), 5-18.

Afshar H (1989) Education: hopes, expectations and achievements of Muslim women in West Yorkshire, *Gender and Education* 1 (3), 261-271.

Afshar H (1994) Muslim Women and the Burden of Ideology, *Women's Studies International Forum* 7 (4), 247-250.

Afshar H (1994a) Muslim Women in West Yorkshire, in H Afshar & M Maynard (eds), *The Dynamics of 'Race' and Gender*, London: Taylor and Francis.

Ali Y (1992) Muslim Women and the Politics of Ethnicity and Culture in Northern England, in G Saghal & N Yuval Davis (eds), *Refusing Holy Orders*, London: Virago.

Allen S (1994) Race, Ethnicity and Nationality, in H Afshar & M Maynard (eds), *The Dynamics of 'Race' and Gender*, London: Taylor and Francis.

Allen S & Macey M (1994) Some Issues of Race, Ethnicity and Nationalism in the New Europe: rethinking sociological paradigms, in P Brown & R Crompton (eds), *A New Europe? Economic restructuring and social exclusion*, London: University College London Press.

Aronowitz S & Giroux H A (1991) *Postmodern Education*: politics, culture and social criticism, London: University of Minnesota Press.

Avari B (1995) Multicultural Education for Adults: rationale, curriculum and process, in I Bryant (ed), *Celebrating Adult Education*, Southampton: SCUTREA, 12-17.

Aziz R (1997) Feminism and the Challenge of Racism: deviance or difference? in H S Mirza (ed), *Black British Feminism*, London: Routledge.

Bains H S (1988) Southall Youth: an old fashioned story, in P Cohen & S Bains (eds), *Multiracist Britain*, Basingstoke: Macmillan.

Bakare-Yusuf B (1997) Raregrooves and Raregroovers: a matter of taste, difference and identitity, in H S Mirza (ed), *Black British Feminism*, London: Routledge.

Ball S J C (1990) *More Means Different: widening access to higher education*, Final Report, Coventry: RSA/Industry Matters.

Baltes P B & Baltes M B (1990) *Successful Ageing*, Cambridge: Cambridge University Press.

Barnes C (1991) *Disabled people in Britain and Discrimination*, London: Hurst & Co.

Barnes C (1993) Participation and Control in Day Centres for Young Disabled People age 16-30 years, in J Swain, V Finkelstein, S French & M Oliver (eds), *Disabling Barriers - Enabling Environments*, Milton Keynes: OUP/ Sage.

163

Barnett R (1988) Does Higher Education Have Aims? *Journal of Philosophy of Education* 22 (2), 239-250.

Barnett R (1990) *The Idea of Higher Education,* Buckingham: SRHE/OUP.

Barnett R (1997) *Higher Education: a critical business,* Buckingham: SRHE/OUP.

Barnett R & Griffin A (1997) (eds) *The End of Knowledge in Higher Education,* London: Cassells.

Barry M (1998) Social Exclusion and Social Work: an introduction, in M Barry & C Hallett (eds), *Social Exclusion and Social Work,* Dorset: Russell House Publishing.

Barry M & Hallett C (1998) (eds) *Social Exclusion and Social Work,* Dorset: Russell House Publishing.

Battersby D (1984) Education in Later Life: what does it mean? *Convergence* 18 (1-2), 75-81.

Battersby D (1990) From Andragogy to Geragogy, in F Glendenning & K Percy (eds), *Ageing Education and Society,* Keele: Association for Educational Gerontology.

Becher T (1989) *Academic Tribes and Territories,* Buckingham: SRHE/OUP.

Belenky M F, Clinchy B M, Goldberger N R & Tarule J (1986) *Women's Ways of Knowing: the development of self, voice and mind,* New York: Basic Books.

Berger P L (1963) *Invitation to Sociology,* London: Penguin.

Bhachu P (1986) Work, Dowry and Marriage among East African Sikh Women in the UK, in R J Simon & C B Brettell (eds), *International Migration: the female experience,* London: Rowan and Allenheid.

Bhachu P (1991) Ethnicity Constructed and Reconstructed: the role of Sikh women in cultural elaboration and educational decision making in Britain, *Gender and Education* 3 (1), 45-60.

Bhachu P (1993) Identities Constructed and Reconstructed: representations of Asian Women in Britain, in G Buijs (ed), *Migrant Women: crossing boundaries and changing identities,* Oxford: Berg.

Bhavnani K K & Haraway D (1994) Shifting the Subject: a conversation between Kum Kum Bhavnani and Donna Haraway, in K K Bhavnani & A Phoenix (eds), *Shifting Identities, Shifting Racisms,* London: Sage.

Bhavnani K K & Phoenix A (1994) Introduction, in K K Bhavnani & A Phoenix (eds), *Shifting Identities, Shifting Racisms,* London: Sage.

Bird J (1996) *Black Students and Higher Education: rhetoric and realities,* Buckingham: SRHE/OUP.

Bocock J & Watson D (1994) Introduction, in J Bocock & D Watson (eds), *Managing the University Curriculum,* Buckingham: SRHE/OUP.

Bonnett A (1996) Anti-racism and the Critique of 'White' Identities, *New Community* 22 (1), 97-110.

Bourdieu P (1993) *The Field of Cultural Production,* Cambridge: Polity.

Bourke J (1994) *Working Class Cultures in Britain 1890-1960,* London: Routledge.

Brah A (1992) Difference, diversity and differentiation, in J Donald & A Rattansi (eds), *'Race' Culture and Difference*, London: Sage/OUP.

Brah A (1994) Race and Culture in the Gendering of Labour Markets, in H Afshar and M Maynard (eds), *The Dynamics of 'Race' and Gender*, London: Taylor and Francis.

Brettell C B & Simon R J (1986) Immigrant Women: an introduction, in R J Simon & C B Brettell (eds), *International Migration: the female experience*, London: Rowan and Allenheid.

Brine J (1999) *Undereducating Women: globalising inequality*, Buckingham: OUP.

Brown P & Crompton R (1994) (eds) *A New Europe? Economic Restructuring and Social Exclusion*, London: University College London Press.

Buijs G (1993) (ed) *Migrant Women: crossing boundaries and changing identities*, Oxford: Berg.

Cain M (1993) Foucault, Feminism and Feeling: what Foucault can and cannot contribute to feminist epistemology, in C Ramazanoglu (ed), *Up Against Foucault*, London: Routledge.

Chapman L (1990) Role Conflict and Role Diffusion: the counsellor in further education, in J Corbett (ed), *Uneasy Transitions: disaffection in postcompulsory education and training*, London: Falmer.

Cherryholmes C H (1988) *Power and Criticism: poststructural investigations in education*, London: Teachers College Press.

Clark A & Hirst M (1989) Disability in Adulthood: ten year follow up of young people with disabilities, *Disability Handicap and Society* 4 (3), 271-283.

Clayton P (1999) Introduction, in P Clayton (ed), *Access to Vocational Guidance for People at Risk of Social Exclusion*, University of Glasgow: DACE.

Code L (1991) *What Can She Know? Feminist Theory and the Construction of Knowledge*, London: Cornell University Press.

Code L (1995) *Rhetorical Spaces*, London: Routledge.

Coffield F (1996) (ed) *Higher Education and Lifelong Learning*: papers presented at School for Policy Studies Bristol University, Newcastle: Department of Education, University of Newcastle Upon Tyne.

Coffield F (1996a) The Resistable Rise of Lifelong Learning, in F Coffield (ed), *Higher Education and Lifelong Learning*: papers presented at School for Policy Studies Bristol University, Newcastle: Department of Education, University of Newcastle Upon Tyne.

Coffield F (1999) (ed) *Why's the Beer Always Stronger up North?* Studies of Lifelong Learning in Europe - 2, Bristol: The Policy Press/ESRC.

Coffield F & Williamson B (1997) (eds), *Repositioning Higher Education*, Buckingham: SRHE/OUP.

Cohen P (1988) The Perversion of Inheritance: studies in the making of multiracist Britain, in P Cohen & S Bains (eds), *Multiracist Britain*, Basingstoke: Macmillan.

165

Corbett J (1990) (ed) *Uneasy Transitions: disaffection in postcompulsory education and training*, London: Falmer.

Corker M (1999) New Disability Discourse, the Principle of Optimization and Social Change, in M Corkier & S French (eds), *Disability Discourse*, Buckingham: OUP.

Corker M & French S (1999) (eds) *Disability Discourse*, Buckingham: OUP.

Crompton R & Brown P (1994) Introduction, in P Brown & R Crompton (eds), *A New Europe? Economic Restructuring and Social Exclusion*, London: University College London Press.

Cryer P (1998) Transferable Skills, Marketability and Lifelong Learning: the particular case of postgraduate research students, *Studies in Higher Education*, 23 (2), 207-216.

Dadzie S (1990) *Educational Guidance with Black Communities*, Leicester: NIACE/REPLAN.

Dadzie S (1993) *Working with Black Adult Learners*, Leicester: NIACE.

Dearing R (1997) *Higher Education in the Learning Society*, London: National Committee of Inquiry into Higher Education.

Deem R (1996) The Gendering of Educational Organisations, in T Coslett, A Easton, P Summerfield (eds), *Women, Power and Resistance*, Buckingham: OUP.

De Lauretis T (1987) *Technologies of Gender*, Bloomington: Indiana University Press.

Delamont S (1996) Just Like the Novels? Researching the Occupational Culture(s) of Higher Education, in R Cuthbert (ed), *Working in Higher Education*, Buckingham: SRHE/OUP.

Department for Education and Employment (DfEE) (1998) *The Learning Age: a renaissance for a new Britain*, London: HMSO.

Directorate General 22 (DGXXII) (1997) *Teaching and Learning, Towards the Learning Society*, www.cec.lu/en/comm/dg22/dg22.html.

Duffy K (1997) Social Exclusion and European Social Policy, in *Empowering the margins: strategies to tackle social exclusion*, Conference Proceedings, London: Southwark Council.

Edwards M (1999) Commodification and Control in Mass Higher Education: a double edged sword, in D Jary & M Parker (eds), *The New Higher Education: issues and directions for the post Dearing university*, Stafford: Staffordshire University Press.

Elsey B (1986) *Social Theory Perspectives on Adult Education*, Department of Adult Education, Nottingham: University of Nottingham.

Episto J L (1994) *Islam the Straight Path*, Oxford: Oxford University Press.

Fairclough N (1989) *Language and Power*, Essex: Longman.

Fairclough N (1992) *Discourse and Social Change*, Cambridge: Polity.

Fairclough N (1992a) The Appropriacy of 'Appropriateness', in N Fairclough (ed), *Critical Language Awareness*, Essex: Longman.

Fairclough N (1995) *Critical Discourse Analysis: the critical study of Language*, Essex: Longman.

Fieldhouse R (1985) The Problems of Objectivity, Social Purpose and Ideological Commitment, in R Fieldhouse, K Rockhill & R Taylor, *English University Adult Education in England and the USA*, London: Croom Helm.

Fieldhouse R & Associates (1996) *A History of Modern British Education*, Leicester: NIACE.

Fine M & Asch A (1981) Disabled Women: sexism without a pedestal, *Journal of Sociology and Social Work* 8 (2), 233-248.

Fish J (1992) An International Perspective on Transition, in T Booth, W Swann, M Masterton & P Potts (eds), *Policies for Diversity in Education: learning for all 2*, Milton Keynes: OUP.

Flowers D & Sheared V (1997) The Signficance of African American Language and Learning in an Adult Education Context: 'going back to our roots', in P Armstrong, N Miller & M Zukas (eds), *Crossing Borders, Breaking Boundaries*, London: SCUTREA, 161-165.

Fordham P, Poulton G & Randle L (1979) *Learning Networks in Adult Education: non formal education on a housing estate*, London: Routledge & Kegan Paul.

Foucault M (1972) *The Archaeology of Knowledge*, London: Routledge.

Foucault M (1980) *Power-knowledge*, London: Harvester Wheatsheaf.

Foucault M (1982) Afterword, in H L Dreyfus & P Rabinow, *Michel Foucault: beyond structuralism and hermeneutics*, London: Harvester Wheatsheaf.

Freire P (1972) *Pedagogy of the Oppressed*, London: Penguin.

Fryer R H (1997) *Learning for the Twenty-first Century*, First Report of the National Advisory Group for Continuing Education and Lifelong Learning, London: NAGCELL.

Geddes M (1997) Social Exclusion in Europe, in *Empowering the Margins: strategies to tackle social exclusion*, London: Southwark Council.

Gilligan C (1979) Woman's Place in Man's Life Cycle, *Harvard Education Review* 49 (4), 431-446.

Halpern D (1998) Poverty, Social Exclusion and the Policy Making Process: the road from theory to practice, in C Oppenheim (ed), *An Inclusive Society: strategies for tackling poverty*, London: IPPR.

Halsey A H (1992) *Decline of Donnish Dominion*, Oxford: Clarendon Press.

Hannan A (1987) Racism, Politics and the Curriculum, *British Journal of Sociology of Education* 8 (2), 119-131.

Hamilton M (1996) Literacy and Adult Basic Education, in R Fieldhouse & Associates, *A History of Modern British Education*, Leicester: NIACE.

Harker R, Mahar C & Wilkes C (1990) (eds) *An Introduction to the Work of Pierre Bourdieu*, Basingstoke: Macmillan.

Harrison R (1993) Learning Later Five Years On, *Adults Learning* 5 (4), 194-5.

Hartley T (1994) Generating Literacy Among Women in a Bilingual Community, in M Hamilton, D Barton & R Ivanic (eds), *Worlds of Literacy*, Clevedon: Multilingual Matters Ltd.

Havighurst R J (1972) *Development Tasks & Education*, New York: McKay.

Haw K (1998) *Educating Muslim Girls*, Buckingham: Open University Press.

Henwood K & Pidgeon N (1995) Remaking the Link: qualitative research and feminist poststructuralist theory, *Feminism and Psychology* 5 (11), 9-30.

Hill Collins P (1990) *Black Feminist Thought*, London: Routledge.

Hockey J & James A (1993) *Growing Up and Growing Old*, London: Sage.

Hooks B (1994) *Teaching to Transgress*, London: Routledge.

Howarth C & Kenway P (1998) A Multi-dimensional Approach to Social Exclusion Indicators, in C Oppenheim (ed), *An Inclusive Society: strategies for tackling poverty*, London: IPPR.

Hughes M & Kennedy M (1985) *New Futures, Changing Women's Education*, London: Routledge.

Hurst A (1990) Obstacles to Overcome: higher education and disabled students, in J Corbett (ed), *Uneasy Transitions: disaffection in postcompulsory education and training*, London: Falmer.

Jackson B & Marsden D (1973) *Education and the Working Class*, London: Penguin.

Jackson K (1980) Forward, in J Thompson (Ed), *Adult Education for a Change,* London: Hutchinson.

Jacobson J (1997) Religion and Ethnicity: dual and alternative sources of identity among young British Pakistanis, *Ethnic and Racial Studies* 29 (2), 238-256.

Jary D & Parker M (1999) The New Higher Education: dilemmas and directions for the post Dearing University, in D Jary & M Parker (eds), *The New Higher Education: issues and directions for the post Dearing university*, Stafford: Staffordshire University Press.

Johnston S & Phillipson C (1983) *Older Learners: the challenge to adult education*, Bedford: Bedford Square Press.

Jonathan R (1993) Education, Philosophy of Education and the Fragmentation of Value, *Journal of Philosophy of Education* 27 (2), 171-178.

Joseph G G, Reddy V & Searle-Chatterjee M (1990) Eurocentricism in the Social Sciences, *Race and Class* 31 (4), 1-26.

Kandiyoti D (1991) Introduction, in D Kandiyoti (ed), *Women Islam and the State*, Basingstoke: Macmillan.

Kassam N (1997) (ed) *Telling It Like it is: young Asian women talk*, London: Livewire, The Women's Press Ltd.

Kennedy H (1997) *Learning Works: widening participation in further education*, Coventry: FEFC.

Khan S (1997) Keeping Up Appearances, in N Kassam (ed), *Telling it As It Is*, London: Livewire Books, The Women's Press.

Knowles M (1990) (4th edition) *The Adult Learner: a neglected species*, Houston: Gulf.

Korsgaard O (1997) Globalisation, Adult Education and Training, in S Walters (ed), *Globalisation, Adult Education and Training*, Leicester: NIACE.

Leicester M (1993) *Race for a Change in Continuing and Higher Education*, Buckingham: SRHE/OUP.

Lloyd M (1992) Does She Boil Eggs? Towards a feminist model of disability, *Disability Handicap and Society* 7 (3), 207-219.

Lonsdale S (1990) *Women and Disability*, Basingstoke: Macmillan.

Lovett T (1982) *Adult Education, Community Development and The Working Class* (2nd edition), Nottingham: University of Nottingham.

Low J (1996) Negotiating Identities, Negotiating Environments: an interpretation of the experiences of students with disabilities, *Disability and Society* 11 (2), 235-248.

Lynch K & O'Neill C (1994) The Colonisation of Social Class in Education, *British Journal of Sociology of Education* 15 (3), 307-324.

Lynch K & O'Riordan C (1998) Inequality in Higher Education: a study of class barriers, *British Journal of Sociology of Education* 19 (4), 445-478.

Mac an Ghaill M (1994) *The Making of Men*, Milton Keynes: OUP.

Majid S (1985) Bilingual Teaching and ESL, *Viewpoints* 3, 11-13.

Marks G (1994) Armed Now with Hope: the construction of the subjectivity of students within integration, *Disability Handicap and Society* 9 (1), 71-84.

Martin J, White A & Meltzer H (1989) Office of Population Census & Surveys, Social Survey Division, *Report 4: Disabled Adults; Services, Transport and Employment*, London: HMSO.

McGivney V (1990) *Education's for Other People,* Leicester: NIACE.

McGivney V (1992) *Motivating Unemployed Adults to Undertake Education and Training*, Leicester: NIACE.

McGivney V (1993) *Tracking Adult Learner Progression Routes*, Leicester: NIACE.

McGivney V (1999) *Excluded Men: men who are missing from education and training*, Leicester: NIACE.

McNair S (1995) Commentary: adults in a changing Higher Education, *Studies in the Education of Adults* 27 (1), 1-8.

McNair S (1997) Changing Frameworks and Qualifications, in F Coffield & B Williamson (eds), *Repositioning Higher Education* Buckingham: SRHE/OUP.

McNair S (1998) The Invisible Majority: adult learners in English higher education, *Higher Education Quarterly* 52 (2), 162-178.

Merton B (1997) Still Disaffected After All These Years, *Adults Learning* 8 (6), 153-154.

Metcalf H (1993) *Non Traditional Students' Experience of Higher Education*: review of the literature, London: CVCP.

169

Milburn F (1996) Migrants and Minorities in Europe: implications for adult education and training policy, *International Journal of Lifelong Education* 15 (3), 167-176.

Mirza H S (1997) Black women in education: a collective movement for social change, in H S Mirza (ed), *Black British Feminism*, London: Routledge.

Moghissi H (1994) Racism and Sexism in Academic Practice, in H Afshar & M Maynard, *The Dynamics of 'Race' and Gender*, London: Taylor and Francis.

Mohanty C T (1990) On Race and Voice: challenges for liberal education in the 1990s, *Cultural Critique* Winter 1989/1990, 179-208.

Morris J (1991) *Pride Against Prejudice*, London: The Women's Press.

Mukherjee T (1988) The Journey Back, in P Cohen & H S Bains (eds), *Multiracist Britain*, Basingstoke: Macmillan.

Mulgan G (1998) Social Exclusion: joined up solutions to joined up problems, in C Oppenheim (ed), *An Inclusive Society: strategies for tackling poverty*, London: IPPR.

NIACE (1993) *An Adult Higher Education: a vision*, Policy Discussion Paper, Leicester: NIACE.

Nixon J (1996) Professional Identity and the Restructuring of Higher Education, *Studies in Higher Education* 21 (1), 5-14.

Oliver M (1990) *The Politics of Disablement*, Basingstoke: Macmillan.

Oliver M (1993) Disability and Dependency: a creation of industrial societies? in J Swain, V Finkelstein, S French & M Oliver (eds), *Disabling Barriers - Enabling Environments*, Milton Keynes: OUP/ Sage.

Oliver M (1996) *Understanding Disability: from theory to practice*, Basingstoke: Macmillan.

Oppenheim C (1998) An Overview of Poverty and Social Exclusion, in C Oppenheim (ed), *An Inclusive Society: strategies for tackling poverty,* London: IPPR.

Parmar P (1988) Gender, Race and Power: the challenge to youth work practice, in P Cohen & S Bains (eds), *Multiracist Britain*, Basingstoke: Macmillan.

Parsons S (1993) Feminist Challenges to Curriculum Design, in M Thorpe, R Edwards & A Hanson (eds), *Culture and Processes of Adult Learning*, Milton Keynes: OUP.

Portside College (1988) *Final Report: 'Portside' College of Further Education Education Support Grant*, REPLAN Project, Department of Adult and Community Education.

Preece J (1996) Class and Disability: Influences on Learning Expectations, *Disability and Society* 11 (2), 191-204.

Preece J (1996a) Positions of Race and Gender: excluded discourses in continuing education, in M Zukas (ed), *Diversity and Development: futures in the education of adults,* Leeds: SCUTREA, 158-161.

Preece J (1997) Gender, Race and Religion: community education and the struggle for cultural capital, *UACE Annual Conference Paper*, Dublin: 1-7.

Preece J (1998) Deconstructing the Discourse of Community Education and Development for Women of Muslim Pakistani Heritage, in P Alheit & E Kammler (eds), *Lifelong Learning and Its Impact on Social and Regional Development*, Bremen: Donat Verlag.

Preece J (1999) *Using Foucault and Feminist Theory to Explain Why Some Adults are Excluded from British University Continuing Education*, Ceredigeon: Edwin Mellen Press.

Preece J (1999a) Making the Curriculum Culturally Relevant Through a Higher Education Core Skills Framework, *South African Journal of Higher Education*, 13 (1) forthcoming.

Preece J & Bokhari R (1996) Making the Curriculum Culturally Relevant: a project in action, *Journal of Further and Higher Education* 20 (3), 70-80.

Purvis J (1991) *A History of Women's Education in England*, Milton Keynes: OUP.

Ramazanoglu C (1993) Introduction, in C Ramazanoglu (ed), *Up Against Foucault*, London: Routledge.

Ransom J (1993) Feminism, Difference and Discourse: the limits of discursive analysis for feminism, in C Ramazanoglu (ed), *Up Against Foucault*, London: Routledge.

Rattansi A (1992) Changing the Subject? Racism, culture and education, in J Donald and A Rattansi (eds), *'Race' Culture and Difference*, London: Sage/OUP.

Raybould S (1964) *University Extra Mural Education in England 1945-1962*, London: Michael Joseph Ltd.

Rieser R (1992) Internalised Oppression: how it seems to me, in T Booth, W Swann, M Masterton & P Potts (eds), *Policies for Diversity in Education: learning for all 2*, Milton Keynes: OUP.

Roberts E (1984) *A Woman's Place: an oral history of working class women 1890-1940*, Oxford: Basil Blackwell.

Roberts E (1993) Neighbours: North West England 1940-1970, *Oral History* Autumn, 37-45.

Roberts E (1995) *Women and Families: an oral history 1940-1970*, Oxford: Blackwell.

Robbins Lord L C (1963) *Higher Education* - Report to the Advisory Council for Education, London: HMSO.

Rockhill K (1996) Challenging the Exclusionary Effects of the Inclusive Mask of Adult Education, *Studies in Continuing Education* 18 (2), 182-194.

Room G (1995) Poverty and Social Exclusion: the new European agenda for policy and research, in G Room (ed), *Beyond the Threshold: the measurement and analysis of social exclusion*, Bristol: the Policy Press.

Saad H (1997) A Model to Combat Social Exclusion, in *Empowering the Margins: strategies to tackle social exclusion*, London: Southwark Council.

Said E W (1995) *Orientalism: Western concepts of the Orient*, London: Penguin.

Sargant N (1992) *Learning for a Purpose*, Leicester: NIACE.

Sargant N (1997) (with Field J, Francis H, Schuller T & Tucket A) *The Learning Divide*, Leicester: NIACE.

Schuller T (1995) (ed) *The Changing University?* Buckingham: SRHE/OUP.

Schuller T (1998) Human and Social Capital: variations within a learning society, in P Alheit & E Kammler (eds), *Lifelong Learning and Its Impact on Social and Regional Development*, Bremen: Donat Verlag.

Schuller T (1998a) Three Steps Towards a Learning Society, *Studies in the Education of Adults,* 30 (1) 11-20.

Schuller T & Bostyn A M (1993) Learners of the Future: preparing a policy for the third age, *Journal of Educational Policy* 8 (4), 365-379.

Schuller T & Burns A (1999) Using Social Capital to Compare Performance in Continuing Education, in F Coffield (ed), *Why's the Beer Always Stronger Up North?* Studies in Lifelong Learning in Europe - 2, Bristol: The Policy Press/ESRC.

Scott P (1997) The Changing Role of the University in the Production of New Knowledge, *Tertiary Education and Management* 3 (1), 5-14.

Shaheed P (1994) Controlled or Autonomous: identity and the experience of the Network: women living under Muslim laws, *Signs* 19 (4), 997-1019.

Shea P (1990) The Later Years of Lifelong Learning, in F Glendenning and K Percy (eds), *Ageing Education and Society*, Keele: Association for Educational Gerontology.

Sherman Swing E (1989) Language and Cultural Rights in the Education of Ethnolinguistic Minorities, *Muslim Education Quarterly* 7 (4), 3-18.

Simon B (1990) (ed) *The Search for Enlightenment*, Leicester: NIACE.

Skeggs B (1994) Situating the Production of Feminist Ethnography, in M Maynard & J Purvis (eds), *Researching Women's Lives from a feminist perspective*, London: Taylor and Francis.

Skeggs B (1997) *Formations of Class and Gender*, London: Sage.

Skilbeck M & Connell H (1996) Lifelong Learning: a missing dimension in undergraduate education, in F Coffield (ed), *Higher Education and Lifelong Learning*: papers presented at School for Policy Studies Bristol University, Newcastle: Department of Education, University of Newcastle Upon Tyne.

Slack S (1999) I Am More Than My Wheels, in M Corkier & S French (eds), *Disability Discourse*, Buckingham: OUP.

Slowey M (1997) A Bridge to the Learning Society, in R Crawford (ed), *A Future for Scottish Higher Education*, Scotland: COSHEP.

Social Exclusion Unit (1998) *Bringing Britain Together: a national strategy for neighbourhood renewal*, www.cabinet-office/gov.uk/seu/1998/bbt/nrhome.htm.

Solomos J (1993) *'Race' and Racism in Britain*, Basingstoke: Macmillan.

Soper K (1993) Productive Contradictions, in C Ramazanoglu (ed), *Up Against Foucault*, London: Routledge.

172

Solomos J (1993) *'Race' and Racism in Britain*, Basingstoke: Macmillan.

Soper K (1993) Productive Contradictions, in C Ramazanoglu (ed), *Up Against Foucault*, London: Routledge.

Stanley L & Wise S (1993) *Breaking Out Again* (2nd edition), London: Routledge.

Swain J (1993) Taught Helplessness? Or a Say for Disabled Students in Schools, in J Swain, V Finkelstein, S French & M Oliver (eds), *Disabling Barriers - Enabling Environments*, Milton Keynes: OUP/ Sage.

Swain J & Cameron C (1999) Unless Otherwise Stated: discourses of labelling and identity in coming out, in M Corkier & S French (eds), *Disability Discourse*, Buckingham: OUP.

Taylor R (1997) The Search for a Social Purpose Ethic in Adult Continuing Education in the New Europe, *Studies in the Education of Adults* 29 (1), 92-100.

Thomas C (1999) Narrative Identity and the Disabled Self, in M Corker & S French (eds), *Disability Discourse*, Buckingham: OUP.

Thompson J (1980) (ed) *Adult Education for a Change*, London: Hutchinson.

Times Higher Educational Supplement (1997) *Rich Pickings: HE success depends on post code*, THES: 18.4.97.

Tisdall E J & Perry C (1997) A collaborative Interracial 'border' pedagogy in adult multicultural education classes, in P Armstrong, N Miller & M Zukas (eds), *Crossing Borders, Breaking Boundaries*, London: SCUTREA, 441-444.

Tuckett A (1996) A Mature Higher Education System? in F Coffield (ed), *Higher Education and Lifelong Learning*: papers presented at School for Policy Studies Bristol University, Newcastle: Department of Education: University of Newcastle Upon Tyne.

Tuckett A (1997) *Lifelong Learning in England and Wales: an overview and guide to issues arising from the European Year of Lifelong Learning*, Leicester: NIACE.

UCACE (1992) Countering Educational Disadvantage, *Working Paper 2*.

University Z (1995) Academic Review Report.

University Z (1994-1995) Minutes and Papers.

Usher R & Edwards R (1994) *Postmodernism and Education: different voices, different worlds*, London: Routledge.

Usher R, Bryant I & Johnston R (1997) *Adult Education and the Postmodern Challenge*, London: Routledge.

Vandenbroucke F (1998) *Globalisation, Inequality and Social Democracy, London*: IPPR.

Van Onna B (1992) Skills Formation in the Workplace, in A Tuijnman & M Van der Kamp (eds), *Learning Across the Lifespan*, Oxford: Pergaman Press.

Volman M & ten Dam G (1998) Equal but Different: contradictions in the development of gender identity in the 1990s, *British Journal of Sociology of Education* 19 (4), 529-546.

Wagner L (1996) Lifelong Learning and the Relationship between Adult and Further Education, in F Coffield (ed), *Higher Education and Lifelong Learning*:

173

Ward K & Taylor R (1986) *Adult Education and the Working Class: education for the missing millions*, Kent: Croom Helm.

Watson D & Taylor R (1998) *Lifelong Learning and the University: a post Dearing agenda*, London: Falmer.

Weedon C (1987) *Feminist Practice and Poststructuralist Theory*, Oxford: Blackwell.

Weeks J (1990) The Value of Difference, in J Rutherford (ed), *Identity: community, culture, difference*, London: Lawrence and Wishart.

Weiner G (1998) 'Here a Little, There a Little': equal opportunities policies in higher education in the UK, *Studies in Higher Education* 23 (3), 321-334.

West L (1997) *Beyond Fragments: adults, motivation and higher education*, London: Taylor and Francis.

Westcott M (1979) Feminist Criticism of the Social Sciences, *Harvard Education Review* 49 (4), 472-430.

Westwood S (1991) Constructing the Future: a post-modern agenda for Adult Education, in S Westwood & J E Thomas (eds), *Radical Agendas? The Politics of Adult Education*, Leicester: NIACE.

Westwood S & Bhachu P (1988) Images and Realities, *New Society* May, 20-22.

Williams F (1998) Agency and Structure Revisited: rethinking poverty and social exclusion, in M Barry & C Hallett (eds), *Social Exclusion and Social Work*, Dorset: Russell House Publishing.

Williamson B (1996) Repositioning Higher Education, in F Coffield (ed), *Higher Education and Lifelong Learning*: papers presented at School for Policy Studies Bristol University, Newcastle: Department of Education, University of Newcastle Upon Tyne.

Williamson B (1998) *Lifeworlds and Learning: essays in the theory, philosophy and practice of lifelong learning*, Leicester, NIACE.

Wilson P (1999) *Lifelong Qualifications: developing qualifications to support lifelong learners*, Leicester: NIACE.

Withnall A & Percy K (1994) *Good Practice in the Education and Training of Older Adults*, Aldershot: Arena.

Woollett A, Marshall H, Nicolson P & Dosanjh N (1994) Asian Women's Ethnic Identity: the impact of gender and context in the accounts of women bringing up children in East London, in K K Bhavnani & D Haraway (eds), *Shifting Identities, Shifting Racisms*, London: Sage.

Young K (1994) Women in Hinduism, in A Sharma (ed), *Today's Women in World Religions*, Albany: State University of New York Press.

Yuval Davis N (1992) Fundamentalism, Multiculturalism and Women in Britain, in J Donald and A Rattansi (eds), *'Race' Culture and Difference*, London: Sage/OUP.

Index

175

177

178